S0-AAE-573

LAUREN ROBERT JANUZ and SUSAN K. JONES

TIME-MANAGEMENT FOR EXECUTIVES

A Handbook from the Editors of
Execu⊕Time®

**Charles Scribner's Sons
New York**

First Charles Scribner's Sons Paperback Edition 1983
Copyright © 1981 Lauren R. Januz

Library of Congress Cataloging in Publication Data

Januz, Lauren Robert.
    Time-management for executives.
    Bibliography: p.
    1. Executives—Time management. I. Jones, Susan K.
II. Title.
HF5500.2.J34   658.4'093   81-16706
                               AACR2
ISBN 0-684-17841-9

This book published simultaneously in the
United States of America and in Canada—
Copyright under the Berne Convention.

All rights reserved. No part of this book
may be reproduced in any form without the
permission of Charles Scribner's Sons.

1 3 5 7 9 11 13 15 17 19 **F/P** 20 18 16 14 12 10 8 6 4 2

Printed in the United States of America.

Some of the material in this book appeared previously in the *Execu-Time* Newsletter and is used with the permission of the copyright holder, Januz Marketing Communications, Inc., P.O. Box 631, Lake Forest, Illinois 60045.

Material on page 32 reprinted by permission of *The Effective Manager*, April 1981, Copyright © 1981. Warren, Gorham and Lamont, Inc., 210 South Street, Boston, Mass. All rights reserved.

Material on pages 167–8 from *The Art of Rapid Reading* by Walter B. Pitkin. Copyright © 1929. Used with the permission of McGraw-Hill Book Company.

Material on pages 173–4 adapted from pp. 22–25 in *Memos for Managers*, by Auren Uris (Thomas Y. Crowell Company). Copyright © 1975 Auren Uris. Reprinted by permission of Harper & Row, Publishers, Inc.

Contents

TIME-
MANAGEMENT
FOR
EXECUTIVES

Introduction

Time is one of life's great equalizers. Everyone—no matter how rich or poor, intelligent or ignorant, accomplished or unskilled—has the same 24 hours a day, 365 days a year. Although this book cannot tell you how to add extra hours to your day or extra years to your life, it can enable you to lift the time-pressure burden from your mind by helping you to train yourself to do more in less time without extra fatigue or loss of effectiveness.

The key to good time management is to work smarter, not harder, in every phase of your life. This applies as much to your method of getting dressed for work as it does to your conduct in an important business meeting. We will give you tips and suggestions for your personal life, home management, interpersonal relationships, telephone use, reading, writing, dictating, getting organized, delegating work, traveling, and much more.

The best things in life may be free, but many people erroneously consider time as one of these free gifts. If you think more clearly about time, you will realize how much value it has for you—just like money—and you will begin to think in terms of spending your time like a careful consumer, to get the best value for it. This does not mean you will eliminate leisure and fun from your life—quite the contrary. By taking a closer look at your time use you can cut the fat from your habitual schedule—get rid of the activities and chores that are not delivering full value for the time spent—and have time left for the things that are really important to you—your career and family.

PRICING YOUR TIME

Before you can fully appreciate the impact that better time management will have on your life, you need to find out just how much your time is worth to you and to your employer. Keep a dollar figure in mind the next time you start a time-wasting activity or slump down for an evening in front of the tube. Just knowing your professional dollar value should help you to focus on what is important—on what is the most productive use of your time at any given moment.

Here is how to price your time the way a financial executive would. Merrill Douglass of the Time Management Center, Grandville, Michigan, says that the first step is to enter your annual salary plus 100 percent for overhead and 40 percent for fringe benefits. Then, add the salaries of your secretary or assistant and your other support staff, if any, plus 140 percent more for their overhead and fringe benefits. Divide this by the number of hours you spend on your key responsibilities. A typical executive spends about one-third or less of his work hours on truly significant tasks.

Here is an example of time pricing. Jerry Radmore is the marketing manager of a company that sells automotive parts by mail. He has an annual salary of $28,000. His marketing administrator makes $13,000, and his secretary's salary is $11,200.

Here is Jerry's time-pricing chart:

His own salary	$28,000
Plus 100 percent for overhead	28,000
Plus 40 percent for fringes	11,200
Support salaries (two workers)	24,200
Plus 140 percent of their wages for overhead and fringes	33,880
Total	$125,280

Divide $125,280 yearly by 52 weeks and the weekly cost of Jerry's time becomes $2,409.23. Jerry spends one-third of his regular business week of 45 hours at key responsibilities. Divide $2,409.23 by Jerry's productive time each week of 15 hours and the hourly cost of Jerry's time is $160.61.

Try this exercise for yourself. Even if you have no support staff and a smaller salary than Jerry's, you will find that your time price is impressive and substantial. Keep this figure in mind, as do professionals such as management consultants, psychiatrists, and others who bill by the hour. Then when you begin a project, you can ask yourself if it is worth your time price.

OTHER PRICES YOU HAVE TO PAY

The concept of spending your time productively can be taken a step further if you keep a few more costs in mind. For example, each uninvited visitor to your office costs an average of $5. Every phone call you take other than during your preset phone time costs $6.50. The cost of picking up a piece of paper is at least 50 cents. If you put it down again without working on it or getting rid of it, that money is lost—down the drain. Each time you stop what you are doing and start something new, it costs you $1.75 on the average, so work on extending your concentration span and avoiding interruptions.

SPEND TIME LEARNING
HOW TO USE TIME BETTER

This book is intended to be an active tool for business people who want to become more effective users of time in their business and personal lives. In it you will find specific down-to-earth suggestions you can put into practice right away, as well as an in-depth analysis of time use that will set you thinking about your overall time-spending habits.

Using this book as a guide, you can improve your ability to do the following:

- Plan for the short, medium, and long run
- Organize your time, your office, and your home
- Deal with others more effectively, including your subordinates, peers, boss, and family
- Use the telephone, dictating equipment, and other conveniences and don't let them use you
- Delegate effectively
- Run meetings well and participate in them to benefit yourself and your firm
- Equip yourself physically and mentally for effective time management
- Take advantage of resources and services that will streamline your time use

Most important of all is the net result: your increased effectiveness as a time manager can bring about a decrease in the stress you feel and an increase in the discretionary time you can spend guilt-free at sports, reading, socializing, and other enjoyable activities (including just lounging around and thinking).

Psychological studies show that the happiest people are busy people. But there are two kinds of "busy"—harried or disorganized busy and calm, effective busy. You can improve your "effectiveness quotient" and become an enlightened consumer of time if you master the basic time-management skills presented in this book.

1.

GOALS AND PLANNING

Where will you be in five years? What steps will you take to get there? These are questions many people shy away from. They fear that setting goals is like "carving in stone," that the inability to live up to a specific goal right on schedule represents a monumental failure.

But such rigid thinking will cramp your style in time management, because goal setting is your first step to effective use of time. It is imperative that you sit down and determine what is important and what can be eliminated, whether you are considering your career or your personal life. Once you have identified the worthwhile parts of your present life and the activities you would like to add or amplify, you can set goals for yourself in terms of maximum time-use effectiveness.

If you are a victim of this "goals-carved-in-stone" fear, remember that we are talking about your personal goals. You need not share them with anyone else if you do not wish to. You are free to modify them or do an about-face whenever you feel it is appropriate.

Keep this freeing thought in mind when you consider your goals. They are your plans to make, work on, and evaluate—no one else's. You do not have to worry about outside approval or disapproval as you set about planning for today, next week, next month, and the rest of your life.

LENGTHEN YOUR TIME HORIZON

How far ahead do you think when planning your day, week, or month? Research shows that most people select a comfortable "time horizon"—one with which they can deal without projecting much into the future—but developing a longer time horizon will serve you well as you plan your time. A time horizon is the amount of time you forecast when considering the consequences of a decision, action, or use of time.

If you are deciding what color pens to buy for your firm's stock room, your time horizon can be short and the time invested in the decision minimal. But if you are considering the addition of a new product to the line that you sell, the time horizon should encompass the entire projected product life cycle. The accompanying time-horizon chart will illustrate some basic examples. The use of such a chart in making decisions will help you to develop the awareness that will lengthen your own time horizon quite readily.

As a general rule, you must look very far ahead when business conditions are quite stable or when your firm would be slow to adapt if conditions demanding change should arise.

In general, your time horizon can be shorter when unpredictable conditions make long-range planning impossible or when your organization can easily adapt—quickly and inexpensively—to any conditions demanding change.

Time Horizon Chart for Charles Hanson, General Manager, Allied Pump Manufacturers

Decision	Years Ahead	Months Ahead	Weeks or Days Ahead
Type of company cars to lease	Years ahead, because the typical lease may be two or three years or more. Anticipate possible changes in amount of car use, trend of gasoline prices, impression you want cars to make, etc.		
Compensation plan for salespeople		Months ahead, because the typical compensation plan is reevaluated annually and can be modified at that time. You would want to consider changing market factors over the year's time, economic climate, territory adjustments, etc.	
Revision of company operations manual	Years ahead, as such manuals are normally modified at long time intervals. The manager would want to consider the long-term effect of revisions to avoid wasting time later if questions were to arise that should have been covered in the manual.		
Schedule of factory workers' overtime			Weeks, assuming such flexible scheduling is understood by employer and employees.

As an exercise in thinking in a longer time horizon, select several decisions that you will have to make. Take whatever time horizon you instinctively feel is correct, and double it. Then see how well you can stretch your thinking into the future for each decision.

As you lengthen your time horizon, you will find that some planning has to be made without all the facts at hand. When this happens, some managers abandon their goal-setting and vow to shoot the rapids and jump right in without a specific plan of action. Such people may claim that their greatest successes occurred without prior planning. What they often do not admit is that some of their greatest failures happened that way, too.

There is a time to gamble, but even your gambling should be planned. Here are some business gambler's tips from a West Coast oil company manager:

Play to win on good new ideas. If you do not, someone else may pull off a coup right under your nose. Plan a sane testing program for the new idea, but do not be afraid to make that test. Commit yourself and your resources.

Stay with a streak. If you are doing well and getting a lot done, do not stop. Take the job one step further and push for the extra result.

Cut your losses. Do not dwell on failure or stay with a sinking ship. Learn to recognize when the odds are against you, and step away to gain perspective so that you can learn from the experience. Then allow yourself some breathing space to "get a roll going" again. Do minor jobs or take time to think and plan until you feel your momentum building once more.

PLAN FOR RESULTS

When stating your goals, think in terms of specific results. For instance, do not say, "Increase sales in 1982." Say, "Increase sales by 25 percent in 1982." And to be more specific, equip yourself with the maximum, average, and minimum results that you can expect from each goal you set.

Then get in the habit of comparing these expected payouts with the time it will take to achieve each goal. To give particular goals priority, you can then determine which items have the highest expected return on time invested.

The result may be a monetary one if you are part of a profit-making enterprise. If you are in a helping profession, the return might be measured in the number of people served.

A positive mental attitude can save you time in planning. Positive thinkers such as W. Clement Stone and Dale Carnegie have much to say that is relevant for effective time planning. For instance, desire is the key: you must want to plan better use of your time.

In his book *The Success System That Never Fails*, Stone explains the magic of desire. If you feel you have stumbling blocks in terms of your attitude toward time management, ask yourself if you really want to be well organized and to use your time effectively. If not, why not? Understanding and conquering your reservations is the key to unlocking your desire to succeed in time management.

Stone suggests that you can develop that desire through three important factors:

Inspiration to action. Understand your need to plan your time better.

Gaining the know-how. Invest the time to read this book to learn the specific time-management techniques that have helped others.

Activity knowledge. Put the know-how into action in your everyday life, and grow from the results.

STARTING TO CHART YOUR GOALS

With this background in goal setting and planning, take some time now to begin charting your personal and business goals. Make sure to give yourself the leverage of a long-term plan in addition to shorter-range goals. Here is why.

A one-week plan can help you get as much as 10 percent more done than you are doing now. What is more, you will begin to recognize those minor crises that caught you by surprise when you did not do much planning.

A one-month plan often increases output by as much as 15 percent. Looking ahead thirty days can help you head off impending crises entirely, since you will recognize them far enough in advance to prevent them.

A six-month plan makes you a dynamic manager. It allows you to recognize new opportunities and make sure you can take advantage of them. In addition, your overall effectiveness is enhanced because you can see which tasks among the many available are most likely to help you reach your long-term goal.

One-, three-, and five-year plans can help you take charge of your career and your life and can direct them so that you can achieve the goals that are most important to you. If you have ever considered changing careers, switching companies, or making other major changes, you need the leverage that such a long-term plan can provide.

LOOK FORWARD, BUT FIRST LOOK BACK

Have you ever written your autobiography? Not for publication, but for self-knowledge? Psychologists suggest that charting your personal history, or "lifeline," can give you the basis you need to begin planning your future. As you think back over your life, try to list your characteristics, values, and state of mind at various stages. Think about the influences that have shaped your life and your attitudes. Then take a piece of paper and mark it to represent five-year intervals of your life to date and to come. Anticipate how long you will live, based on family history and average life expectancy for people of your age, sex, and health.

Start in your childhood, and list on the lifeline you have drawn what you feel to be the landmarks of your life. Do not think too hard about it; the first things that come to your mind are likely to be the most revealing. Once you have done this, take a look at the remaining years of your life. Ask yourself some questions:

- What youthful aspirations have I yet to fulfill? Do I still want to fulfill them?
- How has my career progressed? Am I satisfied with this progression? What goals should I set for the next year (or three years or five years) to make that progression more satisfying?
- Have some of the influences of my early life held me back? What steps can I take to rid myself of these negative influences and move beyond them?

Next, start planning, at least in general terms, what you would like to do with the years remaining in your life. Remember, none of these plans is unchangeable. None of them needs to be shared with anyone unless you choose to do so. But the exercise of thinking clearly and carefully about the time you have to deal with can shed much light on your goal-setting process.

A PLAN OF ACTION
TO MEET YOUR GOALS

Now that you have begun to set short- and long-term goals, here is some specific, action-oriented advice to help you to meet those goals.

More Charts and Less Verbiage

Often something that takes hundreds of words to explain can be presented in chart or matrix form in a clear, easy-to-understand way. Instead of trying to visualize or theorize about your steps toward a goal, try charting your ideas. You will see new relationships that you had not thought of—ways to tie in other departments, projects, and people. Charting your plans gets them off the theoretical level so that you can see holes and anticipate problems.

You will need to develop charts that suit your needs specifically. Important components of such a chart might include anticipated problems and opportunities, a strategy for solving problems and exploiting opportunities, and a checklist of specific steps necessary to meet a goal and the timing of each, along with a listing of who is responsible for each action.

Limited Targeting

If you attempt to set goals to improve every aspect of your business life at once, the task will seem so monumental that you might prefer to do nothing at all. That is why you need to order your tasks and limit your efforts to a single target at a time. Once you have a place for every goal, and every goal in its place, you will find it easier to concentrate on one thing at a time. Your mind will not wander to other goals and problems, because each has its own assigned time and priority.

For example, one week you might concentrate on reorganizing your filing system. The following week, you could zero in on your telephone habits and how to improve them. Never mind that you also want to work on delegation, planning more effective meetings, better dictation, and any number of other time-management skills; each will get your attention when your overall plan calls for it.

To make distant goals seem more reachable, try this four-step method suggested by a purchasing manager in the Southeast:

1. Pinpoint immediate targets you want to hit. (Example: When trying to improve telephone habits, the target may be training your secretary to screen calls more effectively.)
2. Decide on a tangible measure that will tell you when you hit each target. (Example: Assume progress when you have received only one or two unnecessary calls over the period of a week, as opposed to a dozen or more before starting the improvement program.)
3. Create a plan to reach each tangible measure. (Example: Take time to explain the types of calls you want to take automatically, removing fear of failure through discussion of various "what ifs" with your secretary.)
4. Break the plan down into daily action steps. (Example: On Monday, set forth the objective to your secretary, and explain how you propose to meet the goal. On Tuesday, spend some time explaining examples of phone calls you think your secretary can begin handling personally, and how they should be handled, etc.)

A rewarding way to proceed toward big, overall goals is to delineate each successful step with a small celebration of some sort, even if it is only a gift of time to yourself to read a new magazine or to your secretary to take a long lunch hour one day.

Management by Objectives

The term *management by objectives* (MBO) is used frequently today in management circles. It can help you and your staff use time more effectively to meet corporate and personal business-related goals. Here are some MBO time-management specifics.

MBO is a method of tying your firm's profit and growth goals to a set of objectives that each individual can achieve. This system begins with the board of directors and flows down through every level of management and support personnel.

The board of directors sets overall goals and charges the company president with establishing objectives to reach the goals. The president then asks the vice-presidents to prepare personal objectives for their areas of responsibility. Vice-presidents do the same with their subordinates, and so on down through the company structure. The resulting objectives may be charted as a set of supporting actions that reinforce the company's overall goals.

There are several important advantages to the use of MBO. First, MBO encourages employee commitment and involvement. Employees are encouraged to make their own objectives after surveying departmental goals. Because the employees have an important part in planning and decision-making, they are more likely to follow through and do a top-notch job.

Second, MBO gives each employee his or her own area to run. Employees under MBO cannot write off failures and problems as being the result of somebody else's policies. Each employee is "president" of his or her goals and objectives, and each is charged with managing his or her own "company" in the best possible way.

Third, MBO makes regular employee reviews easier and more effective. Instead of a subjective judgment clouded by recent events, an MBO review can focus squarely on measurable performance based on mutually agreed upon objectives and how they have been handled.

Fourth, MBO encourages communication and group harmony. In order to make up individual lists of objectives, each employee must be fully informed about departmental goals and priorities. Managers will have a chance to assess the employee's grasp of the situation based on the objectives put forth for meeting goals.

And last, MBO establishes a solid basis for budgeting and requests for additional funding. The organization of departmental goals and objectives can serve as the base for funding requests. What is more, the exercise of planning will show up personnel and equipment needs, so that they can be met before a crisis arises.

To get started with MBO in your firm, you must take three main steps. Whether your company is a *Fortune* 500 giant or a one-person entrepreneurial shop, you can improve your effectiveness by implementing MBO. Here is what you need to do.

If you do not have corporate goals, make them now. Sit down and make a list of short-term goals, aims for this year, and a plan for five years. Consider all that you control, whether it is an entire company or a one-person department. These company goals will serve as a basis for selecting and implementing your objectives.

Make your objectives achievable but challenging. Remember that you are striving to improve performance. Do not delude yourself by making a goal such as "increase market share" if you know that it is impossible to increase your market share. Strive instead to improve in another area (for example, return on investment). Or look for new product uses.

Write and/or chart your objectives. Involve each employee under you in this. Be positive and enthusiastic about this way of managing, to help insure that each employee is working hard to meet his or her objectives.

2.

TIME-MANAGEMENT EFFECTIVENESS

In order to become an effective time manager, you will need to understand certain characteristics about yourself, and perhaps conquer certain shortcomings. As time-management expert Charles Hamman says, there are no "right" or "wrong" characteristics. The important thing is that you understand what makes you tick so that you can program yourself more efficiently to take advantage of your strong points and soft-pedal your weaknesses.

To get to know yourself from the time-management perspective, consider these questions:

Are you a morning person or a night person? Morning people wake up refreshed and ready to get going. They tend to get up early of their own accord. The hours before noon are very productive for them, but afternoons are less so. This type is often completely burned out by four o'clock.

The night person wakes up slowly and with effort, finally feeling enough in control by 11:00 A.M. to get going with important tasks. The usual 9-to-5 schedule is impractical for this type, because five o'clock finds them just hitting their stride. These types can often work to midnight and beyond without much slip in effectiveness.

Once you decide which type sounds like you, try to discover what your "prime hours" are, and shape your day around them. Even those who have to keep normal office hours can exercise some rescheduling so that the high-priority items are slotted in during peak hours.

Are you task-oriented, or people-oriented? Task-oriented people love to take on knotty, long-term problems that can keep them isolated from others for a long period of time. By contrast, the people-oriented types get bored quickly by paperwork or any long-term job that keeps them away from their associates. These people-oriented workers have a hard time meeting deadlines.

The key to dealing with this characteristic is to make sure your profession fits your personality. The task-oriented person may do well in analytical or budget roles but less well in personnel or sales. By the same token, people-oriented workers should consider the heavy-contact jobs. If you are a task-oriented person who has to sell or a people-oriented type who needs to do long budget reports, make sure you schedule these "foreign" jobs during your peak hours, when you can exert your greatest discipline and concentration.

Are you an intensive worker or an extensive worker? The intensive type finds it easy to concentrate for highly productive short spurts. This intensive activity tends to burn him or her out, so that some projects may not be completed. The extensive person is just as productive, but it takes him or her longer to complete the task. The slow, steady pace means the extensive type does not need as many breaks or layoffs.

Being aware of your intensive or extensive status can help you adjust your pace to any necessary job. The intensive person can learn to schedule regular breaks to avoid untimely exhaustion. In addition, the intensive has to be very sure he or she has selected the most important task to do, because there may not be energy left for another difficult job after the first one is done. Extensives have to make sure they leave enough time to complete the task without rushing.

Are you an A-type or a B-type? The A-type is the compulsive worker, as identified in various research projects on heart attack victims. The B-type is quieter and more deliberative. A-types enjoy activity, while B-types thrive on their relationships, private thoughts, and feelings.

The A-type person tends to do everything personally rather than delegate responsibility. The A-type is often too worried about punctuality and finds it almost impossible to say no. A-types may be guilty of working too much and neglecting needed recreation. If this sounds like you, use your self-control to slow down and take it a little easier. Recognizing the problem should help you guard against its possible consequences.

The B-type needs to guard against procrastination and letting the desk become snowed under with paperwork. Another problem is an inability to stick to a schedule. Once again, self-discipline and self-knowledge are the keys. Understanding the characteristic and the problem can help you take steps to avoid your most likely time-management mistake.

Here are some thoughts for A-types that will help them become more effective:

- Sit tight and do nothing until you have determined who should do what. Do not rush aimlessly from task to task, trying to do everything yourself.

- Work on only the most important activities, and cut out the useless ones.
- Force yourself to go late or not at all to low-priority appointments.
- Make all your calls at once. Resist the urge to pick up the phone when the need strikes you.
- Begin a policy of selective benign neglect. Keep a record of what happens when you neglect certain "sacred cows." Most of the time nothing will happen, and you can eliminate them.

Here are some ideas to help B-types get more done:

- Sit tight and keep working when diversions come along. Give yourself deadlines for each aspect of a job, not just the job as a whole. Spur yourself on to meet the deadlines for the preliminaries, the mid-points, and the final goal.
- Cut down the amount of paperwork you must deal with by delegating it, eliminating the useless parts of it.
- Start a quiet hour and discipline yourself to it. Do not let anyone interrupt you. See pages 191–97.
- Make a conscious effort to cut the fat from your conversations.
- Schedule up to 80 percent of everything you do and refuse to deviate unless an emergency arises.

If you do not recognize yourself as an "absolute" of any of the characteristics above, here is an idea from Charles Hamman. Think back to your younger days, before you mellowed out. Back then you were probably more of a "type" than you are now, since increased maturity may have evened out your temperament.

AVOID PROCRASTINATION

Almost everyone, no matter what type or style of manager, sometimes has problems with procrastination. And, in fact, procrastination can be good in some instances. If you are procrastinating over a project that you feel may not be necessary, the time delay may prove that you need not do it at all. Another plus for procrastination is that while you shudder at the thought of starting that big report, you may find yourself willing to catch up on filing or overdue phone calls that seem too tedious at other times.

But procrastinating too long can be damaging. Each time you put off doing something, it grows less appealing to you. Take a small chunk of the job and do it right away. The rest will then seem less intimidating, and you can schedule it, piece by piece, into your plan.

One magazine executive says, "If I don't do something within the first eight seconds, I know I'm never going to get to it." For maximum effectiveness, start a task the minute you think of it. This does not mean you have to drop everything and do the job from start to finish. But if you at least take a second to outline what needs to be done or to mark a file folder with the name of the job, it will become a part of your open project file, and you will pay attention to it as such.

If you have a hard time getting started on a job, here are some ideas that can get you moving.

Search for the first step. Chronologically, what is the first thing that will have to be done? Identify it and do it.

Determine the longest possible time frame. What part of this problem is likely to take the most time to accomplish? Do this first so that the rest of the project will not be stuck waiting for it.

Search out common bases. What relationships can you see between the pieces of work that make up the project? Use these relationships as a foundation for assignments and plans. Once you have some sort of structure to work from, the project will begin to fall into place.

If you cannot seem to get back to a job that you have started, take a tip from Ernest Hemingway. When he stopped work on a project each day, he always made sure he knew what was going to come next. You can do this, too, when you must leave a project and return to it hours or days later. Make sure you stop on a positive note if you can, and write yourself a reminder of where you will pick up again. This way you will not dread restarting the project; you can look forward to smooth sailing.

SELECTIVE DELAY

There are some good reasons to put off work, but the problem is to determine which reasons are valid and which are not. Here are some guidelines for which tasks to do and which to save for later:

Plant seeds now and save less productive tasks for later. You can plant the seeds of a project by informing one of your subordinates about it and having him or her start the work. This is a better use of your limited time than simply making some notes for yourself or half-completing a purchase requisition regarding the project.

Begin complex projects before simple ones. You can put off one-stage projects. It is wiser to work on those with many steps. And it is better use of your time to work, for example, on a report that will be the basis of an immediate decision rather than on a regular quarterly report that no one reads with much intensity anyway.

Work on the tough projects rather than the easy ones. Put off the simple tasks for your less productive times, and tackle the projects that truly tax your capabilities.

Give yourself a gift of procrastination when you deserve it.

Here is how a financial analyst of a large investment house does this: "As an example, my morning mail usually brings a little brochure or newsletter I have the impulse to read. But it's totally irrelevant to the project I'm working on. Now, instead of reading it, I put it aside and tell myself, 'I'll read that at lunchtime, but only if I've done a good morning's work.' Nine times out of ten my morning will be especially productive, and I'll enjoy reading the piece with a sense of satisfaction, rather than guilt."

INCREASE PRODUCTIVITY

You can adopt a number of methods to help pack more productivity into your day. Among these are effectiveness role modeling, scientific output analysis, searching for the hidden half hour, and several other strategies you can use to keep your day moving.

Effectiveness Role Modeling

As a youngster, you probably tried to emulate at least one older person who embodied characteristics you wanted to possess. Chances are that you learned a lot from it and enjoyed it. The same technique can help improve your productivity if you can identify people in your firm who seem especially effective. Study what they do and what they do not do. Then tailor at least a portion of your management behavior after these role models.

You may want to let them know that you admire their effectiveness and talk to them about the techniques they use. Most managers will be flattered by your interest and be willing to help you.

Do not go too far with this role modeling, though. It is important to remember that your models are human, with their own weaknesses and imperfections. Move on to another source of learning when you have absorbed all they have to offer.

Scientific Output Analysis

When described in scientific terms, time management is the science of increasing output. One way to increase output is to strive constantly to get more out of every minute. Here are some things that successful chief executive officers have to keep in mind:

Output = Concentration + Intensity. If you are preoccupied and allow your mind to wander, output will be cut down substantially. See the section of this chapter on concentration for hints on how to improve this characteristic. Focus on the project at hand 100 percent, and concentrate.

Output relates directly to energy. Factors like tiredness, illness, or a lazy feeling will decrease output as compared with the times when you are strong, healthy, and feeling fit. So invest time in exercise, rest, proper diet, and satisfying leisure activities. They will pay dividends in your effectiveness quotient at work.

Output relates directly to efficiency. Make an effort to cut the fat from your routine. Streamline all your activities, eliminating wasted motion and wasteful, unsatisfying activities. Think through your channels of information to see that everything moves in direct-line fashion as much as possible. The time you spend in this fine tuning will pay off in a more effective use of each minute.

The Hidden Half Hour

Another way to boost productivity is to search out extra time in which to do tasks that you cannot seem to fit into your day. You would know about this hidden half hour already if it were not disguised by something that you now feel to be important. The key is to discover which of your "must" activities are not really necessary and to eliminate them. Here are some hints on how to hunt down the hidden half hour:

- List your current objectives, goals, and targets for the coming year.
- List your current activities in four sections: routines, problems, planning sessions, and all other ways you spend your time.
- Put the two lists side by side and draw a line from each item on the second list to the item or items on the first list that it contributes to. The "orphan" items on list 2—those that do not contribute to obtaining list-1 goals—are your prime candidates for elimination.

If you cut these orphan items out, what would you lose? Probably not much. You may have to keep some of them if they are required by your boss for his or her goals, but the ones that you can eliminate should open up a useful and previously hidden block of time for you.

Sprinting

Carol Davies of Chesterton, Indiana, improves the quality and quantity of her work with what she calls the sprinting concept. She picks a few days in a row, starts early, and works until late in the day with all the speed and fervor she can muster. She does not take time to look back or redo anything. The volume of work she can accomplish is so gratifying that it becomes an inspiration to make her basic capacity higher than it was before.

After four days of sprinting, Carol returns to her normal schedule, which has now become faster and more efficient than before. If she feels that her capacity is beginning to slip, Carol schedules a sprinting session again.

You can try this sprinting technique yourself as a kick-off for your new productivity campaign and keep the idea handy for times when you feel your productivity is starting to drag.

Flexitime

If your firm already has a flexitime plan, you are aware that it is a program that allows individual workers to select their own working hours within certain limits.

Usually there are a few hours each day—say, from 10:00 to 3:00 excepting lunch—at which all employees are expected to be present. But within those limits workers can arrive as early or late as they desire, and leave as soon as they have put in a full day.

If your company does not now have a flexitime program, there are several reasons why you should consider it from a time-management perspective:

Flexitime lets employees choose their own peak working hours. A morning person who hops out of bed at 5:00 A.M. can use that early morning peak time to work from 6:30 to 3:30. The night owl who staggers out of bed at 8:30 A.M. on a work day can still make it to work by 10:00 and stay on the job through his or her peak hours, say, from 3:00 to 6:00 P.M.

Morning bull sessions are eliminated. When everyone is not in at 8:30, the urge to chat around the coffee machine or donut cart is cut substantially. Each employee arrives individually and gets to work without undue socializing.

Commuting is easier. Employees can skip rush-hour train and auto trips if they choose to and thereby avoid arriving at the office annoyed and drained by delays, crowding, and traffic jams.

Flexitime has built-in quiet hours (see also pages 191–97). By setting up definite hours when everyone is in—say, from ten to three—you create built-in quiet hours at the beginning and end of each day. A logical extension of this is to schedule ten to three as permissible hours for meetings and visitors, and keep the before and after hours free for individual work.

Flexitime improves morale. Employees have more control over their work hours and can plan their doctor appointments, childrens' school conferences, and so on, without having to go into long explanations or calling in sick.

Time off is easier to sell to the supervisor when the employee has worked extra hours on the flexible schedule and has time saved in a "time bank."

Flexitime is a plus in recruiting. With flexitime there is no such thing as late anymore, so the time-consuming and rather childish procedure of checking who is late is eliminated. The only criterion for attendance is the total number of hours worked per day or per week.

The findings of *Boardroom Report* in a recent study maintain that 17 percent of private-sector employers now offer flexitime. General results include improved morale and productivity, and reduced absenteeism, tardiness, and turnover. Furthermore, 85 percent of employees would rather work 2 percent less time than have 2 percent more pay, according to a study by the National Commission for Manpower Policy. So the trend away from the "nine-to-five grind" seems firmly entrenched at this point.

Summer Hours

During the summer, many companies go to alternative hours, with either four- or four-and-a-half-day workweeks. Under the shortened workweek policy the staff still works the same number of hours as they do the rest of the year, but they put in those hours in fewer days. Another plan is the four-five-day workweek, which provides every other Friday off as the start of a three-day weekend.

Companies that have tried this summer work style have found it practical from a time-management point of view, because the executive who frequently works a fifty- to seventy-hour workweek anyway will have Friday afternoons, or every other Friday, undisturbed by phones and colleagues.

Some companies cover their switchboards on Fridays with either a recording device or one switchboard operator who advises that the office is closed for summer hours and that the person being called will return the call on Monday.

Maybe you will want to consider such a schedule in your company plans next summer. If it works, you could try it year-round. It is a surefire technique to give the executives more time to get work done without being disturbed by phone interruptions and drop-in visits from staff members.

Peak-Period Staffing

Many businesses carry a full staff all week just so that they can handle the peak of business on one day—for example, Monday if your business relies on incoming mail, and Friday for a bank. Rather than keep a peak-period staff on board all week, why not take steps to level the peaks? Save some of the Monday mail for Tuesday; in most businesses, no great cash-flow problem will develop. For a bank with Friday peaks, try opening Saturday morning and closing Monday or Wednesday. If neither of these ideas is practical, why not hire regular part-timers to work only at the peak times rather than all week.

Perfectionism Cuts Down Productivity

Perfectionists feel compelled to do everything 100 percent right even if it takes hours of extra time and effort that net them nothing. Ridding yourself of these time-consuming habits will add minutes each day and hours each week that you can use to more productive ends. Here are some perfectionist traits to avoid:

Correcting typos. Unless a letter or memo is going to someone of great importance, a slight misspelling will not change your message. It is the point that counts. If you are a stickler, fix the error in pen right on the typed copy.

Redrafting letters, reports, and memos. Learn to dictate them once, and let them fly. Take a few extra minutes to organize your thoughts as you dictate. Or better yet, simply tell your secretary what you want to say and have him or her do the writing for you.

Extreme neatness. Neatness and organization are not synonymous. Your pencils do not have to line up straight, and it is not necessary to purge your workspace of what others might think is clutter. It is not clutter if it helps you work effectively by keeping things easy to locate.

The indispensable person syndrome. You are not the only one who can do your work. And if you are, you would be wise to take steps to change that. Delegate, pass on projects, and share the work with others. Insist that subordinates notify you when it is time to make a decision, a reorder, or a seasonal change, not vice versa. Let go more, and you will be pleased at how most of your people rise to the occasion.

Use a Recession

If your department has been slowed by recession, seasonality, or other dampening factors, you have a fine opportunity to do some organizational work that will reap benefits when you get busy again.

Check work-flow channels. Does work make more stops than it needs to? Do bottlenecks exist? Take time to follow a hypothetical job, step by step, and see what kinks you can iron out or duplications you can eliminate.

Work on your files. Take this opportunity to improve your

files, clean them out, and get them working for you. Send outdated material to storage. You might use the system in Chapter 10 as your guideline.

Nourish your mind. Attend classes, seminars, and other stimulating groups that you do not have as much time for when your business gets busy. Or take the opportunity to study the competition, seeing what you can learn from them.

If you take this advice, you can look forward to improved operations when business picks up again.

PROBLEM SOLVING AND IDEA TESTING

This section will review some officewide concepts and procedures you may use to help get problems solved and save time in the process.

Breakthrough Projects

A breakthrough project is a plan that will yield dramatic improvement over the status quo in a short time. What is needed is a thorough analysis of how time is spent in your office so that you can identify areas where large improvements are necessary and possible. Here are some hints on identifying breakthrough projects:

- Start with a measure of effectiveness, like profit, number of units, or whatever applies. From the bottom up, examine the channels through which your work and/or products flow until you find something that is limiting your productivity.
- If you find several areas where improvement could be made, compare them to find which is the easiest, cheapest, and fastest. The simpler the better.
- Determine the one goal for your first project, and state that goal on paper very specifically—improved

output of a stated percentage or number of units, so many dollars more profit, and so on.
- Get other people involved in the project. Explain the goal and get moving toward it.

You may wonder how such a small change could result in great improvements. The key is to look at your sacred cows objectively and to stop doing the same things over and over without evaluation.

A Way to Pretest New Ideas

The U.S. Navy has a ten-point checklist for pretesting ideas to make sure you do not waste time putting unworkable ones into practice. Here are some questions to ask yourself to see if your ideas will measure up:

1. Will the idea increase production or improve quality?
2. Is this a more efficient way to utilize people than what is being done currently?
3. Will this plan improve operations, maintenance, or construction?
4. Is this plan—if it involves equipment—an improvement over the present equipment?
5. Does this improve safety?
6. Does this idea reduce waste?
7. Does it eliminate unnecessary work?
8. Does the idea reduce costs?
9. Does the plan improve present office methods?
10. Will it improve working conditions?

As you ask yourself this set of questions, keep track of the number of yes and no answers you get. When evaluating the no answers, decide whether the idea will hinder present operations, safety, waste reduction, and the like or merely have no effect upon them. Ideas that have a number of no answers—especially those that create one or more hindrances to present conditions—should be abandoned.

Time-Saving Systems

Attacking problems systematically can help you solve them more quickly and more consistently, according to an article in *The Effective Manager* in April 1980.* Here are four problem-solving steps you can use routinely to make sure your reaction to problems is rational and well thought out:

1. Perceive the problem in clear terms. It may help to verbalize it or to write it down concisely.
2. Organize all available information, recalling past experiences and studying new material.
3. Sleep on the problem; you can often see the answer more easily if you let your subconscious work on it.
4. Test your solution; prove that it is best for yourself before sharing it with others.

You can make sure that your office is conducive to creative problem-solving in three main ways:

1. Open the information channels. Your employees cannot contribute creative ideas without knowing what the issues of the day are. Share with them, and let them know you solicit their help.
2. Diffuse the pressure. Except in times of real crisis, allow enough time for answers to be developed.

* Reprinted by permission from *The Effective Manager*, April 1980, copyright © 1980, Warren, Gorham and Lamont, Inc., 210 South Street, Boston, Mass. All rights reserved.

Ideas created under pressure are seldom as good as those allowed to percolate.

3. Allay fear of failure. Let your people know you would rather that they tried and failed than that they did not try at all.

The *Bank Executives Report* of August 15, 1980, explains several ways to save time in banks through careful organization. We feel these methods have general application for any business.

Every business should have a general organization manual. If you do not have one already, putting one together could be a real time saver if you hire more than a few new employees each year. The function of this manual is to give a new person the big picture of your firm. It should state company objectives and departmental subobjectives. It can also include step-by-step "how-to" instructions for the handling of various tasks.

Having current employees work on such a manual has the added benefit of crystalizing their thoughts on their jobs; they may find that they understand what they do better than before.

A policy and procedure manual is a rules and regulations book to avoid having new employees ask the same questions over and over.

A salary and personnel manual includes information about each position in the organization in terms of duties and responsibilities; current salary level and range; and review schedule. It could also include information on fringe benefits, working hours, lunch breaks, and so on.

Providing new employees with this information will save you and other managers much valuable time that you may spend answering repetitive questions. And having such guidelines written down for them will make your new employees feel more secure and effective in their positions right from the beginning.

Time-Saving Tools

If you use the right tools, you can compress your time just as air is compressed. Here are some of the tools you should use: checklists and comparison ratios; evaluation forms for employee reviews; routine procedures; form letters, memos, and dictating equipment; and reporting forms. All of these items can help you compress your time and efforts by systemizing your work. Rather than starting from scratch each time, you will have a firm base from which you can jump right into the heart of the matter.

Listed below are a few time-saving office products. To find the ones that will streamline your work processes best, leaf through a good office-products catalog or visit the best office-supply store in your area. Unless you have visited such a store in recent years, you may be missing out on some new products that can save you time.

Post-It notes. A new product from the 3M Company speeds message-leaving, flagging pages in books, and adding routing slips to publications. This note paper, called Post-It notes, looks like regular note paper but has an adhesive backing that allows it to be attached to any surface without staples or paper clips. Then the notes come off easily without damaging the surface they have been on. The new notes come in three sizes, the largest being $3'' \times 5''$.

Receipt holder for expenses. This provides the easiest way to keep track of your expenses and make sure you have all the back-up handy. You can order Timesaver Expense Envelopes from the Time-Management Center, P. O. Box 5, Grandville, Michigan 49418. The cost recently was $6.95 for twenty envelopes, each covering a week's expenses for airfare, car rental, taxi-limo, tips, hotel, telephone, meals, parking, tolls, and miscellaneous.

You can also record your location, reason for going, and so

on. Space on the envelope lets you total and recap the expenses for your accounting department. Try a set of these envelopes, or make some up for yourself. They may be just the thing for your entire staff to use—handy for pocket or purse and easy to complete when the trip is over.

Rubber stamps. Get yourself a rubber stamp with your name and address. Better yet, have several for different locations and your home and office addresses. If you write to the same people frequently, have a stamp made up with their addresses as well. Printed self-stick labels are an alternative if you prefer a more professional look. If you do not do either of these things, at least use carbon label sets so that you get four addresses per writing. Your contacts will appreciate labels with your company's address, too. It makes mailing to you much easier.

Timers. Charles Alshuler Company (759 N. Milwaukee, Milwaukee, Wisconsin 53202) makes a handy device you can keep in your pocket and set to buzz when your allotted time for a certain task is up. It is compact and dependable.

Message holder. Here is a tool you can use to keep your telephone messages visible and easily accessible. It is a one-piece plastic clip that attaches to your phone and holds up to several dozen messages. Use it as a telephone tickler file, and get those message papers off your desk for good.

There are many more valuable time-savers available at office-supply stores, so as we suggested earlier, schedule time to take a look soon and get some help in streamlining your office setup.

IMPROVE CONCENTRATION
AND LEARNING SKILLS

You can increase your daily effectiveness if you learn to concentrate more effectively. Depth and time are the two parts of your concentration pattern. Most people require ten minutes to become deeply focused on a project and can sustain that focus for a mere twenty minutes at a time. Then they take a break. This means that within a forty-minute time span, only *half* of the time is spent on concentrated work. The remainder is warm-up or cool-down.

Do your best to build up your concentration span. If you can learn to concentrate for forty-minutes at a stretch, you will have cut your "down" time to 25 percent or less. To get started increasing that twenty-minute concentration span, "stick it out" one minute longer at a time.

Stronger Concentration

Here are some hints that will help you increase your concentration span to as much as three hours or more:

Prepare yourself and your office. Make sure that your surroundings are quiet and your desk is clear. Make a mental commitment to concentration before you begin. Be sure the task you have selected is a very important task that you want to complete. As your eyes and mind wander, make an effort to steer yourself back to the task at hand.

Work in "building block" fashion. Concentrate on a task until you reach a logical, or natural, break. You can do this in two ways. One is to plan step by step how you will complete each task toward the goal and to work on each one for a certain period until it is done. Or tell yourself, "It's eleven A.M., and I'm going to work on this until lunch with no interruptions." Such guidelines and time spans will help sustain your concentration, because you have a specific concentration goal in mind.

"Psych" yourself up. Prime your mind for action by reading or talking over the basics of the project until you understand it thoroughly. Then write down your specific goal for the period of concentrated work—for example, "Solve the traffic flow problem," "Identify the causes for loss of market share," "Find the accounting error." Your concentration period should be the time it takes you to reach this goal.

Pay yourself for improving concentration. Keep a log of your performance at various intervals. How long did you concentrate on various days? How many times each day? Try to identify how long it takes you to reach a state of deep concentration, and work to do this more quickly.

When you have reached a preset goal (for example, doubling your concentration period from twenty to forty minutes or reaching deep concentration in five minutes instead of ten), reward yourself with a present—a night at the theater or a new suit or a day off from work. By continually upgrading your concentration goal and rewarding yourself as each new level is reached, you may be able to increase your concentration span to as much as three hours.

A Concentration Skills Game

Try this timer game suggested by time manager Lance Shaw: Set a timer for several different times of the day. When the buzzer goes off, begin a special period of "ultra concentration." Shaw says, "I use it at the beginning of many work days—for example, to see how much I can get done in the first thirty minutes, the next thirty, etc."

He also finds the timer technique valuable for enforced skimming of the many magazines he must read. He gives himself no more than fifteen minutes on the timer for each periodical. When it rings, he tosses out the magazine and moves on.

Try this new way to bear down for greater concentration and greater productivity rewards.

Layered Learning

Another aspect of concentration is learning more effectively. Performance-effectiveness consultant Bill Eggert suggests "layered learning"—a technique that will help you make good use of otherwise unusable time while traveling, driving, or waiting.

There are many prerecorded tapes that you can use to learn everything from a positive mental attitude to Spanish. Or make your own tapes of lectures, classes, and meetings, and replay them to get the most out of them. Here is how layered learning works:

Layer 1. The first time you hear the material, you get an overview. A few specifics may stand out for you if the tape is quite well written and performed. But by and large, the message will "fade fast" unless you "layer it on" some more.

Layer 2. The main idea of the tape now may become very clear to you, and it will fade more slowly. You will recall more examples and details and be able to relate the high spots of the program.

Layer 3. The details start to stand out for you on the third hearing, and your mind may well begin to function on an active, "how-to-apply" level. Your learning now fades very slowly; it begins to be yours to keep.

Layer 4. With the fourth hearing, the worth of your learning begins to climb quite rapidly for you. You will understand the tape, grasp most of the facts presented, and know the examples and principles that are put forth. You will see applications for the material and begin to apply it in your daily work. What you have learned will stay with you for a good long time.

Layer 5. At this point you will have a full understanding of the tape and its message. The fact that you have participated in so many repetitions has helped burn the material into your subconscious, so that it is always available to you when needed. It has become almost second nature to you.

Try the layered learning technique with a tape or two on subjects you care about. It is a valuable tool that can make down time into productive listening time for you.

DEADLINES

Having definite deadlines is important in time management. Even if you do not have deadlines from your superiors on a project, set some yourself. And let someone else know what your deadlines are; the public awareness will give you that extra bit of pressure to keep you from switching the deadline when the going gets rough. Furthermore, you will get feedback from knowledgeable people who may be able to help you make realistic deadlines on projects unfamiliar to you.

Here are three ways in which deadlines can assist you from a time-management perspective:

Every task deserves a deadline. Even if the deadline is months or years away, assign a definite time horizon for the project. If the task has no deadline whatsoever, it is too easy to put it off. The deadline establishes the project as part of your open file, and you cannot ignore it or shuffle it off. This gives you incentive for completion.

Deadlines versus completion *dates.* Take a look at your track record for meeting deadlines by the completion date set. If you do not meet deadlines well, take steps to study why. Are you being too optimistic, or not taking all factors into consideration? With practice, you should be able to estimate within 5 to 10 percent the amount of time a task will require. And accurate predicting improves time use.

Reward yourself for meeting deadlines. When you hit a deadline right, celebrate. When you miss, analyze the factors that contributed to your failure. Do not let these mistakes happen again. As your number of "deadlines met on time" improves, you will gain confidence and feel more professional. Your fellow workers will realize that you deserve respect and cooperation, since you are a person who gets things done.

If late reports and projects are a problem in your office,

analyze why your deadlines are not being met. Ted Pollock, a time-management expert for the welding industry, has isolated several reasons why you and your people may be late with promised work, and we have added several more:

Requirements not clear. Make sure expectations are spelled out in advance. Do you expect a verbal report or a thirty-page white paper? What does your boss expect? What does your assistant expect? Your other subordinates? Maybe you think the deadline was missed while your subordinate thinks it has been filled with a document or report you considered merely an outline.

Needed time miscalculated. You may be "flying blind" when you set the deadline, especially if this is a first-time project. If that is the case, encourage those working on the project to give their input as to how long it will take and why. Make it clear that you would rather have warning that the project will be late and renegotiate a realistic deadline than have the original deadline missed altogether.

Not enough information to make the goal. Perhaps your subordinate will find that he or she does not know how to go about meeting the deadline, that the steps toward the goal are not clear enough. Again you must encourage openness and try to provide enough preliminary information to get the person off on the right track. Make sure you are available for questions at a scheduled time.

The yes-man syndrome. Perhaps your assistant or subordinate accepts your deadlines without question even if they conflict with other important work. Explain that you would rather hear a no with reasons at the time of the assignment than have the employee miss the deadline or burn the midnight oil for days to meet it.

Arbitrary deadlines. If you set a deadline according to whim, you may give your people too much time or not enough. Deadlines should be far enough away to allow for effective performance, but close enough to insure productivity without padding the necessary completion time.

No allowance for others' deadlines. If your deadline for a monthly report is the tenth of the following month, you will have to make sure all departments that provide pertinent information are completing and disseminating that information in plenty of time. Say the accounting department does not release the previous month's figures until the eighth. If your subordinate's report requires intensive study and manipulation of these figures, your deadline of the tenth may be unreasonable.

Perfectionism. Some workers dislike finishing a project; they like to hold on for more refinements or additions. You need to give specific guidelines as to what the finished project should consist of so that you and your subordinate can agree when it is complete.

Not enough pressure. The word *pressure* may have negative connotations for you. But unless your assignments carry some element of pressure, your people may feel that they can string them out indefinitely. Your task—and it is not such an easy one—is to put pressure on your people right up to the point of maximum return on their time invested.

One way to do this is to change the way you set deadlines. Instead of deciding how long the project should take and using that date as the deadline—or even adding a few days for safety, as many managers do—try cutting down on the time allotted just slightly. Do not cut that deadline too short, though, or your results will suffer as your people get sloppy or come down with anxiety attacks. The idea is to create a challenge, not to frustrate your people or cause them to resent you.

Normally you can allow people from 85 to 90 percent of the time they would ordinarily require to handle an assignment comfortably, and they will be able to produce the desired results in that shortened time without undue stress. But it is important to take individual personalities and attitudes into account. Some people thrive in a pressurized environment, whereas others wilt at the first sign of pressure.

EFFECTIVE DECISION-MAKING

Wishy-washy people do not make good time managers. It is essential to learn how to make a decision and deal with the consequences, rather than wait around hoping decisions will make themselves. You probably can add at least thirty minutes to your productive day if you stop dillydallying and decide faster. The faster and more accurately you can make decisions on what to do, how to handle situations, how to solve problems, the less time you will waste and the less effort you will expend.

Here are some hints that will assist you in making good decisions promptly:

Divide your decisions into categories—"expensive to fix" and "inexpensive to fix." The definition of *expensive* here is not merely monetary but also means expensive in terms of time, manpower, prestige, and the like. Take time to make the expensive decisions accurately, weighing all factors. But do not waste an extra minute on the inexpensive decisions; they are not worth the time. You may even flip a coin!

Thinking about the plan at hand, use this four-part decision-making system: (1) Suppose you decide to proceed. What is the likely result? What is it worth to you and the company? How likely is the plan to succeed? (2) What if you put the plan off? What will be the result of this? Gain or loss? What are the chances of these results occurring? (3) Weigh the possible gains and losses in light of probabilities of their occurring. Compare the alternatives. If one or the other has an edge and you can justify the action it would entail, it will be your best bet. (4) If you cannot find an alternative with an edge over the others, do nothing, but look around for better alternatives or reasons for doing one thing or another.

Keep in touch with the important decision-making criteria around you. What results count the most in your situation? Which results are insignificant enough to ignore?

Review each project in terms of the other items you have at hand at the present. Take an overview and look for the easiest, fastest method of getting all the results you want. Weigh the various projects, and be innovative; you may find a brand-new way of combining projects for exceptional results.

Take responsibility; go ahead and make decisions. Do not kid yourself into waiting for a better time unless it is really likely to occur. Most of the time, doing something is better than doing nothing. Except for projects of paramount importance, speed is just as important as accuracy—if not more so.

3.

PERSONAL ORGANIZATION

When you start the day, the month, or the year without a plan, you find yourself reacting rather than acting—working out of the in-basket on tasks that others provide you with. You find yourself drifting from problem to petty problem and never buckling down to take advantage of opportunities that can yield you and your firm advancement and profit.

Do not allow yourself to become a mere reactor. Take charge of your time right from the start. And except for unavoidable emergencies and surprises, make sure your days and months are planned and implemented *by you*.

WHAT IS YOUR TIME WORTH?

The importance of time planning becomes clear when you price your time, as discussed in the introduction. For added stimulus, try pricing your time at the level you are trying to achieve—that is, a higher hourly rate for yourself, more subordinates reporting to you, and so on.

Understanding the worth of your time in dollars, take a look at your daily activity style. If you see that you need some fundamental changes in the way your office is set up and the way you structure your day, take the time to get organized for good.

OFFICE LANDSCAPING

The way you arrange your office, physically and organizationally, can have an important effect on your time-management efforts. Here are some ideas on office planning and regulation and on materials and equipment that you may find helpful in streamlining your office procedures. In recent years a number of firms have redecorated their bullpen offices into landscaped designs with modular furniture to allow more privacy to clerical workers and better soundproofing. And the modular setup allows flexibility—it can be changed to meet changing needs. However, along with this switch to office landscaping has come, in a number of cases, a crusade to force even top executives to join the modular revolution. Time-management expert R. Alec MacKenzie has identified a number of problems inherent in the modular system—not for clerks but for their bosses: (1) There is not a comfortable amount of room for spreading out files and allowing breathing room. (2) Most of the modular office groupings have walls that can be peered over by taller employees and conversations inside can be heard outside. "White sound"—a low hum—can be programmed into the office to make conversations less audible, and this may be the solution for modular systems with privacy problems. (3) Some of the modular groupings do not have doors, and so the quiet-hour concept (see pages 191–97) goes by the board for good. Proponents of the system say that those who need peace and quiet should go to a special private room set aside for that purpose, but what if many people want that room at once? And imagine hauling all the needed supplies from place to place just for a quiet hour each day—valuable time down the drain.

MacKenzie notes that once, while holding a seminar for employees of a modular office-furniture maker, he brought up objections such as these for the expert reaction. Even those best versed in the field could not counter these problems with workable solutions. When these findings first ran in *Execu-Time,* we received several notes of protest from such furniture makers, but they lacked constructive solutions for the problems cited. So, if you have a modular arrangement in your office, get rid of it or at least improve privacy for those on the executive level. And if someone suggests switching to modular, have your ammunition ready. It is a definite improvement for bullpen workers who would otherwise have no privacy whatsoever, but for decision-making executives it is unworkable.

Interior designer Jack Lowery reports that the way you decorate your office may influence your performance and your employees' performances. He suggests using carpet whenever possible because studies show it reduces absenteeism and creates a more positive feeling than does vinyl tile. It is important also to have enough light; efficiency is increased when eyestrain is eliminated. It is good to have daylight when possible, too, because it is humanizing and has been found to improve performance.

SETTING THINGS UP

Start the day prepared. Getting dressed in the morning should include making sure you have certain essential tools that will save you time all day long. An accurate watch, postage stamps, plenty of change for tolls and phones, cash to avoid emergency trips to the bank, business cards, and pens are necessary items.

Clothing designer John Weitz suggests treating yourself to a very fine pen. It makes a good impression, and you will not find yourself penless because you will not allow yourself to lose track of your investment pen.

Streamline your office. Do you have conversation pieces in your office? Aquariums, artwork, and other unusual items may be attractive, but they encourage visitors to talk about them and not about the purpose of their visit. Time-management expert Ron Davis suggests that you make sure all the signs and pictures in your office relate to company and personal goals. That way, when your eyes wander, you will be encouraged back to work instead of into a daydream. Visitors will have less to digress about and more incentive to be goal-oriented with you when they take in your surroundings.

Set up your office to avoid fatigue. If you set up a specific location for each task you do, you can improve your concentration by creating the right atmosphere, according to time-management trainer Fred Pryor. For example, handle mail from your desk, make your calls from your side chair, and dictate sitting by the window.

The location for each task is not as important as the concept of having a location for each task. This way, when you approach that particular chair or sofa, your mind gets in gear for the task that takes place there. In addition, other distractions will not get through to you as readily in your special place. And when you segment your location as well as your activity, you will find it easier to put other thoughts and jobs aside and to concentrate on the task of the moment.

A good watch is essential. An accurate watch or other time-piece is an important time-saver. You must be able to count on the time as you read it and not waste time guessing whether your watch is three minutes slow or fast. When shopping for that watch, consider the electronic type. Two *Execu-Time* readers had some thoughts on the subject.

One wrote, "I agree that an electronic watch is an absolute must. Mine also has an easy-to-set beep alarm. I use the alarm to keep me aware of deadlines, limit time spent on specific projects (I set it for a two-minute warning), and let intruders know their time is up."

The other reader said, "I bought one of those inexpensive electronic watches (about twenty dollars) with an alarm and chime-on-the-hour feature. The chime helps me keep track of time and politely reminds others who may stop in to chat that I'm concerned about how I use my time. The alarm is a wonderful reminder of the time to get ready for meetings—especially when used in conjunction with my appointment calendar, which lists the materials I'll want to have at the meeting. I've fastened the watch to my pocket appointment book and the tie-in forces me to carry the combo wherever I might bring one of them. This, too, has saved me a lot of time which I used to lose looking for a scrap of paper to jot a quick idea on."

As you learn more and more time-management tools, you may become frustrated because your old systems will be running away with themselves. You see how you could improve them, but it takes all your time just to keep your head above water. If this is the case, you are going to have to bite the bullet and take time to get organized once and for all. Take those files in hand. Clean off your desk and get rid of those distracting knickknacks and pictures. Once you have things organized this way, it will be much easier to keep them in hand. This is important enough for you to cut your lunch hour short or come in early for several days or weeks. Do it now!

TAKE YOUR STYLE INTO ACCOUNT

With a neat office and files in tow (see Chapter 10), it is time to consider your management style. Understanding your style will help you plan your time to maximize your personal effectiveness. You may have a "diffusion" style or a "focused" style. Diffusion style means having a number of irons in the fire at once, being stimulated by having new projects start while others are in midstream or nearing completion. If forced to work on one thing at a time, people with the diffusion style lose concentration and effectiveness: they become bored and stifled. Focused style means zeroing in on one project at a time. A person with a focused style wants to become totally involved; such dedication gives him or her much satisfaction.

If you are a diffusion-style manager, go with your own natural flow. Start new projects while they are ripe, but make sure you have a step-by-step plan to keep them all moving toward your goal. Delegate detail work so that you do not become bogged down on any one project. Keep your options open, but have a detailed schedule for every project and check the progress often to make sure that no project becomes bogged down.

If you are a focused-style manager, your most important task is to choose the one project that will bring you the best return on time investment. Other necessary projects will have to be delegated to others in the department. You can use your natural powers of concentration to keep with the job until it is done and then select another high-priority project. Do not neglect your subordinates, however; make sure you receive regular reports so that you know what is going on with the projects they are handling for you.

UNDERSTAND YOUR PRIORITY CHOICES

Very seldom will priorities be so clear-cut that you can arrange your projects in priority order without hesitation. Here are two tips that will help you determine your priorities confidently.

First, remember that there are two kinds of high priority. Some projects have high priority because you say so and others because someone else does. The priorities set by others will rarely take into account the projects that you are working on. It is up to you to chart all the projects you are to be involved with and to look at them objectively to determine which are really the most important projects.

Second, balance the two kinds of priorities. Objectivity comes in to play again here. If you abandon your own most important projects to take on those of others, you will begin to resent it. But if you ignore others' requests in order to work on your own projects, you will take heat from outside. Ask yourself, "Which one of all the items facing me has the highest relative priority right now?" That is the one you should choose to work on first.

SPECIFIC ORGANIZATION TIPS

If you implement a few of the ideas given below before you do your time log, you may be surprised at what an effective time manager you have already become. If you wait until after you have logged your time for a while, you can implement these hints as part of your first wave of effort to use each hour effectively.

Burnham's plan. Don Burnham, an effective time manager who used his skill to rise to the position of chairman of the board of Westinghouse, suggests this method of organizing your desk each day: He puts all correspondence and notes for each project into a single transparent envelope. Each morning, he stacks a few such envelopes on the desk in order of importance. Burnham takes a quiet hour (see pages 191–97) in the morning, asking his secretary to shield him from calls and interruptions. He works steadily at the first project, then moves on to the second and third if time allows. "The daily priority system is absolutely a necessity," Burnham says. "Without it, there'd just be too many other people and projects competing for my time."

Do two or three things at once. Not always, but sometimes, you can do two or three things at a time if no one thing requires deep concentration or thought. For instance, read mail while you talk on the phone and do some simple note-making and filing. Sign letters while you listen to a subordinate's report. Listen to cassettes while you drive, shave, or enjoy a cool drink on the patio.

Consolidate jobs. Try to get two things done with a single task or action. It sounds simple, but if you are honest you will probably admit that you repeat steps too often without thinking about how you could cut down your trips and time spent. For example, do not run to the copier each time you need copies of something. Save those trips for the time when you would be taking a break anyway and do the copies all at once. Another idea is to listen to the news on an all-news radio station or one that carries local and network broadcasts while you are shaving or driving to work. You will cut out the need to read a newspaper. Or have a meeting and eat lunch while you confer.

Cheat on your watch. If you tend to be late, set your watch ahead five minutes or an hour. Every time you check it, you have that added cushion of time. And thinking about the cushion will remind you that time itself is valuable.

Organize and reorganize. Organizing and reorganizing may seem like a waste of time to you, but Norman MacRae, deputy editor of the *Economist,* says that regular cycles of centralization and decentralization can be of great value. The emphasis on organization keeps effective use of time as a paramount goal at all times. Reorganizing can be one very good way of rooting out ineffective procedures and habits ingrained through years of use and of replacing them with well-conceived, cost-effective ones. You can implement this idea by scheduling periodic reorganizations of parts of your operation; try a different departmental reorganization every three to six months. Reassign tasks so that more people will learn them. Restructure reporting relationships and work groups. Move people from office to office if you think this will help. The whole process will encourage people to think through the systems and methods that they take for granted and perhaps find faster, cheaper, better ways of achieving goals effectively.

DEALING WITH INCREASED WORK LOAD

The way that you handle increases in your work load indicates your grasp of time-management techniques. Some people respond with longer hours, eliminated lunch hours, and a tense, high-pressure push, using the same old procedures that have been used for years. The result? A work week growing to fifty, sixty, or even seventy hours, with no relief in sight.

Time managers, however, take the time to think about this new work load first. Say that you have been supervising ten people and suddenly you have a new, additional group of five to oversee. The old-style manager would increase supervisory time by 50 percent to accommodate 50 percent more people. But if you streamline, delegate, and think through the situation, you should be able to supervise the fifteen people in the same time it took you to oversee ten. Here is how: Look at the work load differently. Instead of a multiple of the same old work load, look at this new addition as something that puts you in a higher level of management. Instead of using the methods you used in the past, look for new ways to get all your work done in the same time you spent before. This may involve upgrading your subordinates so that you can delegate more to them. It can also mean working with others in your department to find more effective procedures and systems.

TIME WINDOWS

If you understand the "time windows" concept, you can use it to open up new blocks of time for yourself, time you never knew was at your disposal before. Catching a plane provides an example: If you make the plane, you are on schedule at that point. If you miss it, you cannot catch up—the time window is blocked until you get off the next available plane. Time windows like this are always opening and closing for you, but it is up to you to learn to recognize them.

Say that you are trying to finish an important project one day and a "must" meeting with another executive is coming up, one that should yield answers that will allow you to finish the project. Because of schedule limitations, the two of you can get together only at 10:00 A.M. this morning, or next Thursday at 4:00 P.M. If you seize the opportunity to meet today, you can jump through a time window and complete the project. If you wait until Thursday, a window will close in front of you. And the fact that you let the time window close may mean that you will miss other windows before Thursday.

Another way to think of time windows is as a series of traffic lights. Try to hit the green lights any time you can. If you get stopped at a red light, you may find yourself having to stop at every one. But if you speed up and get through an amber light—finishing something faster than you normally would, for instance—you may be able to catch the next four or five green lights easily.

Practice this technique by taking a simple project and listing the steps from beginning to end. Point out the various time windows coming up and date them. See if you can get through all the windows on time.

As you work on the project, note any additional time windows that you did not anticipate. Figure out what will happen to your project for each window you miss. Make sure you get through at least the key windows on time, and see how much your work flow and tempo increase.

TIME LOGS

The best way we know to get a handle on time use is to watch it like a hawk for a week or so. That way, you will see how much of your time is going down the drain and how much you are able to spend effectively.

Your time log can become the basis for a serious time-reform program. You can read time-management theory only so long without having a specific time chart of your own to help you put some changes into effect.

If you get bogged down in logging your time, you will be destroying the time-saving benefits of a time log. Find a method that is quick and easy so that you can note your time use without wasting too much attention or energy on the task. One way is to use a preprinted diary form with hours printed along one margin. Keep notes on what you do and when, throughout the day, beside the various time notations. Or make a grid listing the activities you usually perform on one margin, and cross-reference this with five-, ten-, or fifteen-minute time intervals. Then all you need to do is put a check mark in the right box for each time interval. If you forget to do this on time, try setting a buzzer for every fifteen minutes. Turn it off, make your check mark, and you will be back to work.

Our Recommended Time Log and How to Use It

The daily time log on page 57 will help you find out how much time you are spending each day on trivial items versus prime items. Keep it for a week or longer, until you are thoroughly convinced that it is a good record of how you spend your time. In other words, if an all-day meeting is part of the first week you log and this is very unusual for you, you might want to add a day or two to the log to make sure all your normal activities are reflected properly. Here are your instructions (see the sample log illustrated):

1. Draw up a list of activities and projects that you are likely to do on a regular basis. Include specific projects (the Smith proposal, the Jones report, etc.) as well as routine or general categories (weekly staff meeting, daily discussion with boss, etc.). In addition, list your everyday activities (i.e., telephone calls, writing and dictating, interruptions, instructing staff, reading, thinking and planning, waiting).

2. Take a copy of the time log form you have completed and fill in your projected activities and projects along the top. Decide whether you will log at five-, ten-, or fifteen-minute intervals. (This will depend upon how much you jump around in your work.)

3. Keep your original time log for a few days as practice. At each interval, put a check mark in the column that describes what you have been doing.

4. The Comments column can be used to help you remember the details of what you do. After a few days you will find that some of your headings are not necessary and you will want to add others as you need them. But whatever headings you use,

make sure you mark them every five, ten, or fifteen minutes as you have set up the log. Do not wait until lunchtime or the end of the day, when you will get a distorted picture.

5. After your test days, redo your form with the headings that you ended up with. Photocopy five copies of this new form and use it for the next five days of work.

6. With the five days' log in hand, begin your analysis of time use. By category, how is your time spent? What projects are the biggest time users? The smallest? How does the amount of time compare with the results you achieve? What are you doing that you could stop doing? What should you be spending more time on?

7. After completing your analysis, do a time log for one particular project. Record the time used for each facet of the project with detail and accuracy. Strive to eliminate wasted time and expand the productive periods involved with the project.

8. Once or twice a year, repeat your time-log routine and do a project log or two. This will keep the time-use analysis skills fresh in your mind and help you to keep from slipping back to old and wasteful habits.

The time log is a fact-finding tool that will help you see where you are tossing time out the window and where you are using it wisely. Once you have completed the analysis, use it to help you budget your time and spend it where it will yield the best results.

Allocating Your Time

The first thing you may notice as you go over your time log is how much time you allocate frivolously. For exam-

TIME LOG

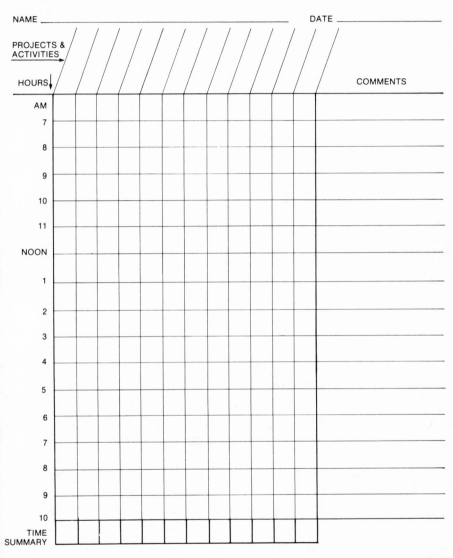

NAME _____ DATE _____

PROJECTS & ACTIVITIES

HOURS | COMMENTS

AM
7
8
9
10
11
NOON
1
2
3
4
5
6
7
8
9
10
TIME SUMMARY

Instructions: Each 5, 10, or 15 minute interval (by the clock),
place a √ in the column that best describes your activity.

Copyright © 1978, 1981 Jan5z Marketing Communications, Inc.

ple, is it really necessary for you, personally, to spend hours per week on something like tours of the plant? Are you spending a full ninety minutes on routine correspondence, things your secretary or assistant could probably handle for you?

To rid your schedule of some of these time-wasters with low payoff value, consider your priorities, your job description, and your goals. If any activity fails to further or fulfill these three considerations, get rid of it.

When a new project is proposed to you, count up the total time commitment over its lifespan—not just the immediate time involved. If you must take it on, find some time space in your schedule by eliminating low-yield activities.

Time Logs for Your Subordinates

You can multiply the value of time logged by getting all your subordinates to do it, too. Do not shove it down their throats, though, because that way you will see what they think you want to see on the sheets or they will fake the sheets or avoid doing them at all.

The easiest way to involve your subordinates is to make the project a group one, shared with you. You do your time log first and analyze it. After a few weeks, call your subordinates together and show them what you have learned about yourself.

Suggest the time-log system for their use, but make it clear that their results will not be used against them in any way. Admitting your own time drains and exhibiting evidence that you have plugged them after doing the time log should help you to convince your people to try this technique with you.

MORE HINTS FOR PLUGGING TIME DRAINS

Zero-based time budgeting. The managing director of an investment firm wrote *Execu-Time* with this suggestion:

"I've adopted the zero-based idea to my time-management effort. In other words, from time to time I start from 'ground zero' and re-evaluate all my time use. At the beginning of every quarter, I run a time log and find out where my time is going. Then I ask myself, 'If I weren't already doing this, would I start now?' If the answer is no, drop it. If yes, I calculate how much time that item deserves and limit my involvement to that much and no more. In this way, I prevent myself from wasting valuable time on activities and projects that don't really warrant the expenditure."

Break some pesky time habits. A great deal of what you do is habitual, so if your time log shows that you are wasting time, habit may be partly to blame. Here are some suggestions on how to change your habits:

Make yourself aware of your time-use habits. Think especially of all those automatic parts of your day, such as commuting, taking breaks, and moving from one task to another. Ask your associates for help in spotting time-wasters.

Make it your goal to break at least three time-wasting habits and replace them with new, more efficient ones, such as finding a better route to work or starting to take the train so that you can read while commuting. File things immediately instead of letting them pile up. Or rearrange your work day so that you start with an important project instead of reading the mail or the newspaper.

Add up how much time these new habits save you. If you find that the time saved is worth the effort, make a note to try some more streamlining on a month-by-month basis.

Make sure your office is ready. Clear out your office last thing before you leave at the end of the day so that you do not have to spend the first part of the next day finding something to work on. Set out just one important project on your desk, and file everything else by priority and subject. This will spur you on to start the day with that top-priority project.

Use a time log in reverse. An administrator of a large West

Coast city proposed this idea: "I found the time log so useful for keeping track of my time, I decided to *use it in reverse*. I plan out my schedule to the minute, at least a day ahead of time (I leave 20 percent unscheduled for flexibility). Then as I go through the day, I check every half an hour or so to see if I'm on time. If I'm not, I speed up or move to the next item to get back on track. If I am, I pat myself on the back and keep plugging. At the end of the day, I've done everything I planned to, and sometimes quite a bit more."

TO DO TODAY

The "To Do Today" sheet is a comprehensive planner that will help you use your time effectively each hour of the day. The form on the next page is one you can size to suit your needs and copy for use on an everyday basis. (Forms are available by the pad from *Execu-Time*; write P. O. Box 631, Department 0192, Lake Forest, Illinois 60045, for more information.)

This form can help you take your time-log results and mold them into a more effective daily performance scheme. The "Tasks" section is used to note each item that requires some action from you during the day. You can rate your "Priorities" from 1 to 5 or A, B, C, depending upon your preference. It is important to attack your tasks in the assigned order of priority.

Put a time for completion in the "Deadline" column for each task you take on. Also make an estimate of the amount of time it will take you to do the task. This will help you schedule your hours and also serve as an exercise to help you become a better judge of how long things take.

Among items of equal priority, do first the items that have to be completed earliest. You can also select from among these equals to find the job that fits the amount of time you have left in the morning, afternoon, or day after your high-priority work is scheduled.

TO DO TODAY

NAME _____ DATE _____

PRIORITY	CLIENT/TASK/JOBS	TYPE	DEADLINE	ESTIMATED TIME				√	PHONE CALLS (name, purpose)
									- - - - - - - - - -
									- - - - - - - - - -
									- - - - - - - - - -
									- - - - - - - - - -
									- - - - - - - - - -
									- - - - - - - - - -
									- - - - - - - - - -
									LETTERS/REPORTS TO WRITE

PEOPLE TO SEE/DISCUSSION TOPICS		ACTIVE PROSPECTS		Follow-Up	
					LONG RANGE (task, when due)

Copyright 1979, 1980 JANUZ MARKETING COMMUNICATIONS, INC.

Execu·Time   P.O. Box 631 • Lake Forest, Illinois 60045
All rights reserved.

As you complete each item, cross it out to give you a sense of accomplishment and to make sure you do not waste time re-reading completed items. You might want to use a highlighter pen to do this or make a thin cross-out line so that you do not lose track of what you have accomplished by obliterating it.

Use the "Results and Actual Time Used" column to note exactly what results you achieved (for example, delegated to Sam, signed contract, ordered new machine). Note how long it took you to complete each item and check it against your estimated time to help you to improve your estimating power.

During the day, keep your To Do Today sheet close at hand. Make a note of phone calls you want to make, people you need to see, and letters you need to write. Do not stop what you are doing to call, visit, or write in response to the needs that you have noted. Write them down and forget about them until the proper time. Then do all—or as much as you can—of these tasks at one time. Do your best to note all topics you need to discuss with a certain person, points to cover in a letter, and so on. This will keep you from calling, visiting, or writing more than once.

Use the "Long Range" column to note items needing future work. At the end of each week, transfer these "futures" to a "tickler" file. (See Chapter 10 for more on this.)

At the end of the day, transfer the items that were not completed to a new To Do Today sheet for the next day. Each Friday, make up sheets for each day of the following week, and outline the important projects that need to be done, slotting them into the time schedule. You can touch up the day's schedule the evening before you use the sheet.

Take satisfaction in what you accomplish. When you look over your To Do Today sheet at the end of a day, do not bemoan the fact that every item is not completed. Perhaps there were unforeseen and important interruptions that kept you from your schedule. Whatever the reason for not completing each task, turn your attention to what you did complete.

After all, you will never completely wipe out the list, future tasks and all. If you could, you would not be an executive; ongoing projects are the name of the game for those in higher ranks. Gain your sense of achievement from the steps you were able to take toward your goal.

If the daily-plan concept is new to you, do not despair. Studies show that as many as 70 percent of executives seldom take the time to make a daily plan for themselves, although they know that such a plan is a definite asset.

Here are some hints that will help you get the daily planning task down to as little as five minutes, an investment of time that will yield impressive dividends in terms of what you accomplish during the day: (1) *Plan only what you think you can accomplish.* It will not help to overschedule yourself and try to cram a week's work into a day's plan. (2) *First things first.* Schedule your highest priorities first, allowing two or three hours in the morning for an important project and a few hours in the afternoon for the same or a different high-priority job. Fit your additional work into the chinks created by this work schedule. (3) *Allow extra time.* On paper, a task looks as if it should take an hour and a half to complete. But allow yourself about 10 percent more time than that—say, an hour and three-quarters. That way, you will feel good if you complete the job in an hour and a half and you will have a bit of spare time for unexpected things, for reading, or for other work. If the project does take longer or if someone interrupts you, you will have a cushion to keep you from getting too much off schedule.

Use That Daily Plan

Here's how to use your daily plan in practice, as tasks come up:

Consult the plan before you start a task. Does this job fit in with your day's plan? Is now the proper time to make that call or write that memo—or should it be noted and done later?

Keep the plan on your desk or pin it on the wall in front of you. It is a map or focal point for your day, and you should be able to refer to it often.

Score your performance at the end of the day. On a scale of 0 to 100, how effective were you, and how much did you accomplish from the plan? Try to upgrade your average as time goes on.

Make long-term plans, too. How about trying weekly, monthly, quarterly, or yearly plans? Use these as the skeleton on which you build your daily plans. Over the years your plans can become benchmarks and performance goals for your entire career.

Keep those plans as a permanent record of what you did and when and as a record of your accomplishments. Look over your accomplishments when you feel useless and dragged out, and you may get a lift.

The Nuts and Bolts of Daily Planning

List the parts to a whole. Instead of marking down a big project by name on your To Do list, list the parts that will add up to the whole. For instance, do not just put down "monthly report." Instead, mark things such as "collect financial data," "obtain sales figures from marketing," and so on. That way, you will view each specific part as a manageable job in itself, and you will have the whole project organized right from the start.

Rubber stamps simplify your To Do form. Instead of recording daily or weekly routines by hand, time after time, either get yourself a set of rubber stamps for recording "staff meetings," "association luncheon," and the like or have your To Do Today tablets printed with these items on them.

Do not let your systems overlap. Does your To Do list overlap with other reminder systems like a notebook, calendar, or set of random scrap notes? If so, you are wasting time in two ways. First, you are overorganizing. Second, you may forget to check all of your sources or forget where an important note is located. That is why we suggest one master system for time management, preferably a portable one if you are in and out of the office a lot. Notes that you make at home can be entered into the master system in the morning. And make sure your system extends far into the future so that you do not lose track of upcoming appointments and plans.

To Do Today sheets do not have to be white. Some people like white To Do sheets, but others find that a bright color will keep their attention better focused on that important daily guide. Ask your office supply house for paper color ideas that are attention-getting but not harsh.

Schedule time to be creative. A danger in using a To Do form is that you will schedule all your time for specific, active jobs and not allow yourself any time for creativity and kicking ideas around. Productive time is a "must," of course, but it must be supplemented by creative time, time to prepare, and "overhead" time to keep up with paperwork and other chores. You need to achieve a proper mix among these categories.

The more time you spend in creative thinking, the more you will achieve in your other activities. For instance, if you take the time to create a new procedure to eliminate a task, you will generally get better benefits than by trying to do the old task more efficiently.

Writers and artists have always insisted upon having time to be creative—to think or even daydream their way to new ideas and concepts. And it is not a luxury for a business executive to expect the same.

A number of top managers make it a regular part of their plans to think, daydream, and let their minds rove to long-term goals and dormant ideas. If you think you do not have time for this, try scheduling it on that To Do list. Harvard studies show that the highest achievers dream and fantasize constantly about how to achieve their goals. Do you owe yourself any less?

Departmental To Do Today sheets. If a number of you work on the same projects, you may wish to serve your whole department with a To Do Today list. A blackboard or other large bulletin surface will work as well. When someone completes a job, he or she can scratch it off and mark his or her initials and time finished.

To lunch or not to lunch. What should you schedule for lunchtime on your To Do Today sheet? Time managers are divided in their views on lunch. You will have to fit your position on lunchtime activities to your personal style and preference.

A top film industry manager says, "I have one rule I never break: 'Don't eat lunch alone.' Even a one-hour lunch wastes 5.2 weeks over the year. So I take a lot of people to lunch to talk business and make deals. It not only saves my time, it gives me the edge, because a man with a full stomach is usually a pushover."

The opposite view is to take a quiet hour (see pages 191–97) at lunchtime, since almost everyone else will be out of the office. Have lunch a bit later or earlier than most people—11:00 A.M. or 1:30 P.M.—when the restaurants are not crowded and you can get quick service.

One thing the experts agree on: do not skip lunch. Eat something nourishing, even if you just do it at your desk. The morning buildup of stress can put you into a frenzy by early afternoon if you do not give yourself a break at lunchtime.

So if at all possible, get outside and smell the roses—get a new perspective on things to carry you through the afternoon. Well-chosen nutritious foods can supply the energy you need, especially if you tend to burn out in the afternoon.

Quickie tasks. As you plan your day, you will find some spare minutes—right before lunch, for example, or between the completion of a task and the time a visitor is to arrive. Time chinks will show up during the day if you complete a task ahead of schedule or if the visitor is a bit late. That is why you should have some "quickie tasks" at the ready so you can use those spare moments to the fullest. In five or ten minutes you can complete a decision that you have put off, review a file for an upcoming meeting, write a letter or two, read some paperwork, or take a relaxing walk or coffee break.

In just one minute you can jot down a note about a new idea or arrange upcoming tasks. It is easier to find little jobs like this if you keep a file or stack of them handy. Soon you will find that you can clear out dozens of these quickie tasks each day using only the time tidbits you have wasted in the past.

TELEPHONING

The telephone, like the television, is a modern convenience that serves an excellent purpose for communications. But also like the television, the phone may cease being a convenience and make slaves of its users.

Do you get out of the shower to run for the telephone the moment it rings? Do you hurry up the steps and unlock the door to run in and grab the phone if it is ringing when you get home? At the office, do you interrupt someone who is visiting you on a long-standing appointment to take a call from someone who just decided to ring you up? Do you pick up the phone when a thought passes through your mind, instead of tending to your high-priority projects and putting off the phone call until the proper time? If you do, you are quite typical: you are a victim of telephone tyranny. Unless you recognize the hold that the phone has over you and take steps to modify it, you will lose a lot of time catering to Ma Bell's device.

Here is how a sales engineer put it when he wrote to us:

> Why is it that people will answer the telephone under most any circumstances—convenient or not? People jump out of the bathtub, interrupt conversations with scheduled visitors, stop on their way out to important meetings to answer that insistent jangle.
>
> I've quit doing these things—but I don't miss anything important. I have a telephone-answering machine at home, and at the office my secretary is trained to screen all calls and save all but the most vital for my intensive 'phoning period' each day. Then when I sit down at the phone with my stack of messages, I can get them all out of the way at once instead of breaking my concentration many times.

This engineer has outlined an effective preliminary plan to eliminate telephone tyranny from your life.

SELECTIVE DIALING

Do not just cut down on your phone calling in an attempt to reduce phone-time waste; you may find you've cut some essential communications. The telephone is one of your best time savers if you use it properly. Here is how to set yourself up for selective dialing:

Think before you dial. Get out of the habit of reaching for the phone every time it occurs to you. Ask yourself whether calling is the most time-effective step at this moment. Do not make the call in circumstances where, for example, you are going to have to follow up with confirming paperwork anyway, or the person you are calling will not be able to give you an answer until after he has had a period of thought and/or consultation, or several people are going to have to approve the item you are calling about before you can get into action.

In circumstances like these, what is the good of an immediate phone call? You can scribble or dictate a note and get the ball rolling at your convenience instead of interrupting your train of thought—and that of the person you would be calling —for a phone call that may get diverted to unrelated topics.

Do not mix business calls with pleasure. Many people have the habit of conducting business on the phone for a minute or two and then saying, "So, how's everything?" or "How have you been?" You can almost feel the climate of the call changing from business to socializing. And you do not have time for much of this chitchat if you are going to finish your To Do Today list.

If a business associate you are friendly with starts this personal chitchat routine and you do want to talk at some point, just say, for example, "I'd love to tell you all that's been happening, but I'm swamped at the moment. How about lunch next Wednesday?" (Or substitute a tennis date or whatever you usually do with the person.) Set the social date, then get off the phone and back to business or you may be in for a thirty-minute bull session that can put your whole schedule out of whack.

If a supplier or other person you do not have outside social contact with starts in with chitchat, simply answer that openended "How's everything" question in this way: "Everything's fine, but really busy. I'd love to chat, but I must run. Thanks for calling." Take the initiative, and politely but firmly end the call.

Save up your calls for your telephone times. Without even thinking about it, most of us take our calls as they come in, no matter what is being interrupted. Did you ever notice how clerks do this at many department stores? There may be only one clerk in the department, with five customers lined up, but when the phone rings, as often as not a clerk will leave the customers standing there, purchases in hand, to answer the phone immediately. Meanwhile, those purchasers may become so disgruntled that they will drop the goods they meant to buy and walk out of the store.

When you have carved out time to concentrate on a report, to see a long-awaited supplier with a fine new product, or even to take your well-deserved fifteen-minute break, why should you answer the phone just because it is ringing? If you have no secretary or assistant to field the calls, take turns with an associate, to allow each other quiet hours. Or get yourself a phone-answering machine. The several hundred dollars it costs will save you much more in time spared from the tyrannical telephone.

Schedule a telephone hour. Collect your list of calls during the day, and have your secretary help you gather all relevant material so that you do not have to get up and search through files as you are talking. Have some paperwork or reading at your side to fill in time while waiting to be connected or for initialing and skimming during your routine calls.

When you are prepared, do nothing but make calls for a solid hour. You will find that you get a momentum going and that you will not talk very long to any one person, because you have a number of calls to make in the time limit you set. Furthermore, by saving up your telephoning for one period each day beforehand, you can list topics you want to discuss with each person you call.

Some executives suggest making calls first thing in the morning so that you can reach people before they become busy and thus eliminate many call-backs and unreturned calls. You will also be set to do work that depends on the results of your phone calls. You will be gratified with the amount you accomplished at one sitting without interrupting your carefully planned work schedule.

Do not hold indefinitely. Make your own policy about how

you will treat being put "on hold." You can refuse to be put on hold and call back later in your phoning period. If you decide to remain on hold, especially to reach someone who is hard to get by phone, keep some paperwork or reading handy so that you will not simply stare into space while waiting.

If the party you are calling is out, leave a precise message. This may save your having to call back. Make sure the message-taker gets your full name and phone number, the purpose of your call, and the type of response that you expect. In many cases, the message-taker can relay the message and get the answer for you.

Do call before you travel. Confirmation calls can save you an amazing amount of useless travel time. Always call before you leave for appointments to confirm the date and time, and get good directions. Find out the agenda of the meeting to make sure that you do not leave without any necessary materials. Your call could uncover the fact that the reason for the meeting is now a moot point, enabling you to stay at your desk instead.

Practice winding up conversations fast. Here are some closing gambits you might try: "I know you have lots to do, so I'll let you get back to work now"; "Look at the time. It's been great talking with you, but I must go. Bye!"; or "Well, if that winds things up I've got to get moving. I'm expected upstairs at a meeting."

TELEPHONE DISCIPLINE

If the whole concept of selective dialing and weaning yourself away from constant phone use is difficult for you, here are some discipline hints you can try on yourself:

Log your calls. Just as you log your time use to see where your hours and days go, do the same with your telephone calls for a few days or a week. List time, purpose, and duration of call. Check how many calls contain an undue amount of personal conversation. How many did you pick up in the middle of important, concentrated work? Get a handle on your own phone use and phone time-wasters. Understanding this will help you to discipline yourself.

Do not answer the phone yourself. Train your assistant or secretary to take your calls and to handle and make most outgoing calls. Pick up the phone only when someone you must talk to is already on the wire—but do not keep him waiting. (It is not cricket to be a time-waster for someone else.)

Give your secretary or assistant three separate lists of people. First, those you do not want to have put through to you. These could be people you will call back later or perhaps ignore. Second, those you will talk to when they call except during conferences or scheduled quiet hours. Third, those you will talk to whenever they call. You should revise these lists often so that the person who answers your phone feels confident with them.

An extra note for those who take your messages: ask them to spell the names phonetically as well as with the regular spelling so that you will pronounce the names correctly when you call back. This tip is especially important for people in sales or service.

Let people know when you are not available. For the convenience of those who call you often, do your best to schedule your quiet hours (see pages 191–97) and unavailable time and keep to them. Let these frequent callers know when the best time to reach you is—or if they want to call and leave a message, when you will call them back during your regular phone hour.

Make notes before you get on the phone. Outline your calls, and you will save time when you pick up the phone. Those you call will appreciate your organized presentation and questions. Take notes while you are talking to make sure that you have your assignments right and that you and the other person agree on what was decided.

PHONE SHORT CUTS AND SERVICES

A number of conveniences are available to people who use the telephone frequently. Most of them are inexpensive when you consider the amount of time and aggravation they can help you save. Talk to your telephone service representative about conveniences available through your phone company. Others are available commercially, most often from the larger office-supply firms.

Here are some of the devices and services that may help you use the phone more effectively:

Touch-tone phone. The simplest phone time saver of all is the touch-tone phone. You can dial by touch-tone in about two seconds, compared with several times that long as you wait for the dial phone to spin its way around seven times.

Speed dialer. If you make a lot of phone calls—especially long-distance calls with many numbers—you can save time by using a speed dialer. For one hundred to two hundred dollars, the machine stores, selects, and dials more than thirty phone numbers. You can get the same service from the phone company in many areas for a small monthly charge. Each use saves you the time of looking up and dialing numbers.

Call waiting. If you have not checked recently with your local phone company about new services, you may find that they now offer this option. Call waiting allows you to take a second call on your single phone line and put the first call on hold. You can switch back and forth at will. You can also get a feature in many areas that will allow you to set up your own conference call with two calls coming in on your phone. This is especially helpful for those who work at home or for small businesses with just one phone line.

Call forwarding. This is another service that phone companies are offering in many areas. If you are working at home for the day and do not want to miss your important calls, you can use this feature to have your calls ring at home just as if they were ringing at the office. By punching a simple code into your phone and then dialing the number where you will be, you do not have to miss a single call.

Telephone amplifier or headset. The phone company offers an amplifier that lets you have your hands free while you talk on the phone. You simply talk normally, and the speaker picks up the sound of your voice and transmits it. The voice of the person on the other end comes back to you through a speaker. It is a small unit that takes up very little desk space.

Some of your callers may object to the amplifier for two reasons: it cuts down on privacy and makes the person using the "squawk box" sound as if he is talking from the depths of a cave. So if you prefer, you might like to look into a light-weight headset, a much lighter version of what switchboard operators wear. Try your favorite office-supply store, and look for one with a long, elastic cord to insure mobility.

Phone timer. A senior partner in a Wall Street law firm provided this tip: "We can afford lengthy phone conversations, even to Timbuktu. But I still keep my little three-minute timer next to my phone, and I rarely go overtime. If I have something lengthy to say, I would confirm it in writing anyway. So now I just write, and if I call in addition, it's just to say my letter is coming and to ask for a prompt reply."

A sophisticated version of a phone timer is called the ITT Timer Phone. It is a special device that starts timing your call from the moment you lift the handset. The elapsed time ticks away on a red digital display so that you are constantly aware of how long you have been on the phone. For more information on this, you may write The Drawing Board (256 Regal Row, Box 220505, Dallas, Texas 75262) or check your local phone company for other sources.

Message center. Take and place all messages in a special location for easy access when your call-back hour rolls around. Make sure that your secretary, assistant, or whoever may give you messages while you are away knows about this central place.

Answering machines and services. If you are a one-person operation and have no one to shield you, you should consider one of these alternatives. If you opt for the answering machine, get one that makes it easy to change your message on a daily basis so that you can customize the message and take care of answering an expected question or two right on the tape. An answering service is more expensive in the long run, but more personal. Take your choice.

Telephone charge card. You can save yourself the aggravation of scrambling around for change in airports and stations by obtaining a charge card. Anyone with a phone can get one by contacting the phone company. Another advantage to having a charge card is that you will receive an automatic record of the calls you placed, as opposed to those you paid for in cash, for which there is no record. Also, when you have a charge card, it is easy and convenient to make long-distance calls at a friend's home or office.

Conference calling. You may not be aware that you can set up a conference call—usually in a matter of minutes if all parties are available—simply by dialing the operator and asking for the conference-call operator. This can be much less costly in time and money than traveling to a meeting.

For bigger conference calls, a firm like Darome Connection may be able to help you. Darome offers a sixty-line teleconferencing system that allows you to hold a meeting of employees from Maine to California. Participants can either call or be called. If they join the conference before it is over, they will not disrupt the meeting. They can call and join the meeting at any point. A roomful of people can participate by using special teleconferencing units, too. No prior scheduling is necessary. To find out more about the service Darome offers, call toll-free (800) 243-0991.

Cordless phone. This "freedom phone" can be taken all around your house or office—even to the bathroom or out walking the dog. It works anywhere within 300 feet of a base station that you set up where you want it. For more information, contact the Electra Company, (800) 428-4315; in Indiana, call (800) 382-1076.

5.

FACE-TO-FACE
CONVERSATIONS

Often when an efficiency expert or time manager is portrayed in movies or television, the person is characterized as a snippy, snide individual with no time for personal conversation or friendship. If you have let that image of the efficient manager cloud your impression of how well time managers interact, this chapter should be a pleasant revelation to you, because it explains a way of communicating that is cordial, positive, friendly and still encourages effective use of time.

As one of the correspondents of *Execu-Time* said, "I used to worry that effective use of my time would cut me off from my people and make me a 'cold fish.' But in practice, I find effectiveness and courtesy go hand in hand. With my time under better control, I feel less resentful of the time I give to others.

I can convey my honest respect for people now in much less time than I used to spend keeping up pretenses I didn't feel."

Canadian management consultant Peter Buetow points out that efficiency in most offices is considerably lower than on assembly lines, but without the regular pace of machines and quotas, the office workers' foot-dragging does not show up as readily. Buetow warns that formal meetings are not the real time-wasting culprits but rather the two-person encounters involving small talk, waiting while the other person takes a phone call, even taking time for a coffee break before getting down to business. Guard against this by saving up an agenda to discuss with each person at a specific time. Avoid "drop in" one-on-one meetings.

GET INTO THE MEAT
OF THE CONVERSATION

Charles Ford, an author, lecturer, and consultant on organizational behavior, analyzed eighteen typical executives in fourteen companies to see how they spent their conversation time. These men and women spent an average of 5.5 hours per day in meetings, dictation, phone calls, and other means of conversation. The study showed that about two hours per day per executive were wasted in what Ford calls "conversational fat." How did these executives blow 2 hours per day, 10 hours per week, 520 hours per year? Ford says the fat breaks down into the following four main types. Hints on avoiding such fat are included.

Irrelevant conversation. Chitchat before a meeting is an example of conversational fat. Granted, a bit of chatter helps start the flow of business conversation, but it should be limited. Most of us allow ourselves to become involved in far too much of it. Suggest saving irrelevant conversation for later. Say, "I'd like to hear that, but I'm late for an appointment right now. Can we talk about that later today or tomorrow?" If you use this ploy, you will find that the topic hardly ever surfaces again.

Extra background data. Nonessential background data often comes from those who want you to know how much blood, sweat, toil, and tears it took to bring a project to its conclusion. Such information is interesting and informative, but not really necessary. You may well have heard it already. If presented at all, it should be in written form to be read later—or better yet, prior to the meeting—by those who are interested and may need the information. When a speaker begins telling you extraneous background, a polite way to sidestep it and get right to the heart of the matter is to say, "I know you've put a great deal of hard work into developing this, but can you tell me the status right now?" This way, you acknowledge the efforts of your colleague so that he or she knows you appreciate the work that has been done. And you are being cordial in cutting through to the business at hand so that he or she will not lose face. You will probably get the short answer you want after using this technique.

Digressions. Ford calls this tangential conversation. It happens when the discussion leader loses control and talk goes off in all directions. Several people may be talking at once. For example, you might ask, "Where should the new copier be located?" Someone else starts talking about the traffic flow on the west side of the office, which leads to a discussion of the location of the lunchroom, which leads to talk about how the candy machine prices went up last week, which leads to general discussion of the climbing cost of living, and so on.

A meeting leader has to keep the topic on target, perhaps by using an easel with the question posted on it. The leader of the group could tap the easel when the conversation begins to leave the subject. The chief executive of a machine tool company used this technique, according to Ford, with excellent success. As time went on, he had to tap the easel less and less often as those in the meetings learned to stay on the subject.

Supporting information. This may come from the same people who wanted you to have extra background data. They will tell you every last point they ever considered to get to their conclusion—if you let them. Whereas the background data usually has to do with what others did or did not do, this supporting information most often has to do with the speaker's own activities. Once again, you may need to know this material, but it should not be hashed over in a general meeting. If distributed at all, it should be in written form.

Listen to yourself next time you are in conversation. How much of what you say is verbiage that no one would miss? If you are like most of us, you will find that more than a third of the words you utter are fat. It takes time and effort to rid your conversation of those sinister extra phrases. You have to be alert to your own unwanted fat. Notice the fat level of the conversation of others in your office. Most firms have a conversational fat level that is considered normal, Ford says. You may be able to reduce your own fat level, but you will have to enlist the help of others to speed up the communication process on an officewide basis. Many people load up on the supporting information to build credibility for themselves and show how hard they have been working. If you acknowledge this, and then ask a question that leads right to the bottom line, you can short-circuit the long-winded supporting speech. Say something like this: "Charles, I know you've been very much involved with the project. On the basis of your findings, tell us now how many desk tops you think we can sell next quarter." See the table on the next page for an indication of how to cut the fat.

COMMUNICATE RIGHT THE FIRST TIME

Sometimes the short-term gain when you give instructions too quickly is a long-term time-waster if the person you

Fat versus Lean Conversation

Fat Conversation	*Lean Conversation*
I would like to begin by telling you the marketing assumptions for the report that will follow. . . .	The marketing assumptions for this report are. . . .
We're here today to discuss the color selection for the painting of the executive washroom. Speaking of which, did you hear the one about the salesman who. . . .	Today's topic is paint color selection for the executive washroom.
Let me tell you how we reached this conclusion . . . (followed by a blow-by-blow report).	The conclusion we have reached is . . . (specific, concise conclusion).

are communicating with did not catch exactly what you meant. So take the time to communicate correctly the first time:

Give feedback. To make sure you understand what others mean, ask, "Are you saying . . ." or "If I understand you right, it's . . ." That way you can make sure you are interpreting things correctly, the way your associate meant for you to hear them.

Give clear instructions. Include the specific goal or objective involved in the job in your instructions. Make sure the person you are dealing with understands the deadline and the means you want to have employed. If they are taking the job step by step, set up a specific time for them to report and receive the go-ahead for the next step.

Encourage questions, and listen to them with care. If the

questions are inappropriate, you may find that you are not getting through to the person. You should try a different way of approaching the topic. If the questions are relevant, answer them fully and ask the person if the answer is clear. Leave plenty of time for understanding, and you will save time in the long run. This way you will not be interrupted later with questions you can get out of the way now, at one sitting.

Have the person repeat the instructions. If you are receiving instructions from your boss, repeat them to make sure all is clear.

Summarize conversations and meetings. When things are winding up, give a summary of what was agreed, who will do what, and when any relevant deadlines or future get-togethers will be. Make sure the summary is accepted by the others, as it will be the basis for future action.

YOU DO NOT ALWAYS
HAVE TO BE RIGHT

How much conversation time have you and others in your organization wasted arguing points of little or no importance? The desire to be right and to win the argument is the ultimate time-waster. Instead, try to build on the things you and your colleagues agree on for a productive experience without repetition and amplification of arguments.

Another time-waster along these lines is the debate over who is at fault for a delay or mistake. Those "he said, she said" discussions quickly bog down into cat-and-dog fights that can leave permanent employee-relations problems. Refuse to let such discussions get started in your department. Get down to the business of the problem at hand and how best to solve it.

COMPROMISING WILL NOT SAVE TIME

The foregoing discussion may lead you to believe that compromise is the best answer to resolution of divergent views.

In fact, conventional wisdom says that compromise does save time by cutting down on discussion and disagreement.

But management expert and author Robert Townsend contends that while compromise solutions merely keep things calm, they may not be in your firm's best interest. So do not compromise; make definite decisions when your role is supervisory. Listen to both sides and select one or the other. That way, the winning side will feel responsible for shepherding the project to success. And make sure the losers realize it's okay to lose a battle once in a while.

6

MEETINGS

Meetings are the number-one scapegoat in modern time management. They are blamed for being a timewaster; a platform for long-winded, ego-driven speakers; or a disorganized forum that confuses more than it elucidates. But the fact remains that most of us in business will need to call and attend meetings at least some of the time, to get business organized and to disseminate important information on a face-to-face basis. Meetings can also serve as a way to get to know the people you work with, especially if you work most of the time on a long-distance basis.

The human elements of a meeting can help you to sense a feeling in the group and to build a team spirit among the participants. The short bits of social talk before and after the meeting add richness to business life and keep people from feeling like mere automatons. But meetings are expensive, so plan and use them right.

THE COST OF MEETINGS

Keep the cost of your meetings under control by figuring your time investment. Add up the salary costs of all those who will attend. This is about 24 cents per minute per $10,000 in annual salary. Now add the opportunity costs of other work these people might be attending to if they were not in the meeting. A good estimate of this would be twice the person's salary, or 48 cents per minute per $10,000 salary. At this rate, a meeting of five people who make an average of only $15,000 a year costs you $3.60 per minute! And do not forget travel time, coffee time, irrelevant conversation, and all the other extras that eat up those minutes at $3.60 a crack.

Keeping the dollar figure of your meetings' cost in mind will help you to keep your meetings on track. You might share the cost figure with those you are meeting with or even post it at the front of the room to deter people from digressing and making long-winded speeches.

THE MEETING AGENDA

The meeting agenda is one of the most important factors in success. Here are some guidelines for preparing and using agendas:

Issue an agenda beforehand. Do this two or more days in advance of the meeting to allow people time to prepare relevant material.

Itemize the points that you want to cover.

Prepare the points in question form. Indicate who is responsible for the answer. You will get answers that result from careful thought, not off-the-cuff comments that tend to take more time and contain less meat.

Put the points of the agenda in the exact order in which they will be covered. Resolve the key issue on each point before you move onto the next point, and do not let the meeting wander from topic to topic. Check off each item as you move on.

Allocate meeting time, minute by minute, to each item in advance. Stick to this schedule no matter what, to avoid digressions and conversational ploys. Remember Parkinson's Second Law: If other things remain equal, meeting time will be spent on items to be discussed in inverse relation to their importance.

If you would prefer not to discuss the food in the employee vending machines for an hour and have only ten minutes left for the new profit-sharing plan, try this minute-by-minute scheduling technique.

COMPONENTS OF AN EFFECTIVE MEETING

Top executives and their subordinates were surveyed to determine what a meeting needs most for effectiveness. Here are the results:

A strong leader. The leader must keep the meeting moving ahead briskly, with each topic where it should be, everyone involved, and decisions being made.

A meaningful purpose. Do not hold a meeting because it is Tuesday and you have a staff meeting every Tuesday. Make sure there is a clear and important reason for the meeting and that you have a specific objective to achieve.

Privacy. Petty phone calls and messages should not interrupt the meeting. The room should be quiet and away from activity so that concentration will not be broken.

A select attendance list. Keep it as short as possible. Invite everyone only if the meeting is to disseminate information or to start thought processes. If you are going to analyze a situation or reach a decision, eight people should be the maximum.

PARTICIPATING IN MEETINGS

Here are some pointers to help you maximize your own efficiency regarding meeting attendance and participation:

Reduce the number of meetings you attend. Try cutting down 10 percent to start, and try to work up to an 80 percent reduction bit by bit. Decide which meetings to attend on a consistent, sensible basis, such as importance, personalities, sequence, distance, and topic.

Meet with yourself. A Red Cross field officer gave this idea to *Execu-Time*: "My calendar was frequently so full I had no time alone for projects that needed to be done. Part of the problem was the numerous meetings for which I was scheduled. So I got the idea to schedule meetings with myself for those necessary but neglected projects. When an interruption threatens, I can honestly say, 'Sorry, but I'm scheduled for a meeting then.' "

If you are not chairman, keep the minutes. If you volunteer for this job, you are likely to get it. Now you can focus the discussion and avoid digressions, because you will have a right to ask questions such as: "Are we still on agenda item 3? Have we decided who is going to do what, by when?"

Limit the amount of time you spend at any one meeting. Leave long-winded meetings early, or slip in late if the meat of the meeting comes at the end. Walk out when the first repetitions start, especially if people are repeating worthless points. Explain, if you must, that you have to make an important phone call or handle an emergency item. Then go back to the meeting later if it is still going on. Or better than that, send your assistant or secretary to cover for you and explain that "something important came up."

Bring a tape recorder. You can record the main meeting points while you allow your mind to wander. People are likely to give you extra credit for being thorough, while all the time you will be working in your head or on paper, if possible. The trick is to keep your face attentive and to tune back in every so often to make a comment that indicates your interest.

Learn what you can about the people who are there. Find out how they think, how they react, what their strength and knowledge is. Get to understand their personalities and reactions. This information may come in handy later when you need to work with these people outside your own department.

Ask what the meeting's purpose is when you arrive if there is no agenda stating it. During the meeting, ask for the purpose as many times as you need to in order to keep the discussion on track. If those in charge cannot state a purpose for you, get up and leave immediately.

Demand competent leaders. If a meeting is out of control, your time will go right down the drain. When the meeting leader is incapable of putting the group on track, you may decide to help out, leave, or ask for a better leader to take over. You will be able to upgrade your meetings by having everyone who attends fill out a simple leader-evaluation form at the end of each meeting. Each form should carry the date, time, leader's name, and areas for the attendee to rate the leader on effectiveness of meeting, conservation of time, and significance of meeting outcome. After a number of people have taken their turns as leader, collate the forms and compare. Soon your best meeting leaders will rise to the top, and you can give them the authority to lead most meetings from then on.

CONTROLLING MEETINGS

Here are some guidelines to help you make sure you are a competent meeting leader:

Decide on a purpose. Meetings may be called for problem solving, for planning, for training, or for making announcements. Sometimes two of these reasons may be combined—for example, a first section for exploring possible problem solutions and a second section for final decision-making.

Establish the best people–energy ratio. Generally, the more people you invite, the more energy you will have to exert to make it a good meeting. Limiting attendance creates an "in-group" who feel privileged to be there and who will work to retain their status as part of the group.

Avoid meeting tardiness. Boardroom Reports suggests that if meeting tardiness is a consistent problem, take aggressive action. Let the minutes show who is present and who is absent. Record who arrives late. At the next meeting, make sure the minutes are read when the offenders are present.

Keep meetings argument-free. Do not let adversaries sit across the table from one another. If certain people tend to bog down your meetings with their discussions, seat them apart and on the same side of the table. Lack of eye contact will kill much of their ability to keep fighting.

Use speed minutes. Instead of having everyone take notes and divert attention from the speaker by trying to scribble everything down, appoint one person to take "speed minutes" of the meeting. The one chosen should be knowledgeable in the area being covered. The speed minutes should cover only the decisions, assignments, deadlines, and other items that people feel should specifically be on the record. To supplement such speed minutes, you might try taping the meeting and simply keeping the tape on file for legal and other purposes. Do not have the tapes transcribed; just keep them on hand in case something specific needs to be pursued later.

Some time managers even write out minutes in advance of the meeting and add notes or changes on them while the meeting takes place. Photocopies can be made so that everyone will have a rough copy of the speed minutes before he or she leaves the meeting.

Control the discussion. You can maintain control through the following:

1. *Positive or negative feedback.* Expressions, movements of the head, body language, and verbalization all tell others what you think of the discussion. Use feedback to guide the discussion along a fruitful course.

2. *Focus.* If your questions are general, the focus of the meeting will remain broad. When you ask specific questions, the meeting will focus on specifics. Tighten the focus as much as you can to bring about an ultimate conclusion.

3. *Recognition.* A nod, a pat on the back, even raised eyebrows become a powerful salute in the enclosed atmosphere of a meeting. If you write a note on your pad, it is as if you were applauding the speaker. On the other hand, glazed eyes and a look of boredom punish the speaker. Interrupt that speaker and your objection becomes even more specific. Ask someone else a question and you will virtually shut off debate on the old topic.

4. *Summaries.* Each time you summarize the action, you can close the door on a portion of the meeting and open the door to the next part. If you do not like an opinion or option that has been discussed, simply exclude it from the summary.

5. *Conclusions.* If you feel it is time for a definite conclusion, keep focusing and pressing for an end. If you think more study and work should be done, simply unfocus the discussion by generalizing; this will leave the question open for later conclusions that may be better.

Determine the best time and place. Studies show that a morning time in a quiet, comfortable location is best for problem solving and planning. If your goal is to tell news or to train, hold short in-house meetings. The time of day is not of real importance. If news or training meetings will take a half day to a day or more, hold them elsewhere to avoid interruptions. Monday morning is a terrible time to hold a meeting. If you must have a regular meeting each week, try Wednesday. It is not close to the pre- or postweekend slow-down period that may affect meeting attendees.

Bunch your meetings. You can actually stack meetings like pancakes and save time you used to waste. Put two to five short meetings back to back on your schedule and you will have a knot of activity that flows fast and effectively. Get all those meetings over in the morning, and you will have an afternoon left for other important work. For example, schedule meetings for 10:00, 10:40, 11:00, and 11:25. Allow time to cover only what must be covered. At the start of each meeting, explain that you have another meeting scheduled in that very room at a certain time. Ask your associates to help you be sure to conclude the present meeting in time for the next one. (You can use this technique with appointments, too. If you do, you will have a polite and honest reason to get visitors to leave when their business is concluded.)

End on an up beat. Especially if you feel the meeting may have dragged on too long, make sure you provide an upbeat ending. Pick out a satisfying item—a problem that is easily solved or a report showing progress or profit. Then take a few minutes to restate assignments and deadlines, including definite instructions on what must be done before the next meeting and at the next meeting.

Schedule future meetings. A professor thought up this one for *Execu-Time*: "At a meeting, it's easier and faster to schedule the next get-together if you bring a supply of transparencies with blocks of time marked off. Everyone gets one and crosses out times he is unavailable. When you stack the transparencies and look through, you can see immediately when everyone's time is clear."

ALTERNATIVES TO MEETINGS

Sometimes there is a more time-effective way to handle a situation than to hold a meeting, especially if travel is involved. Here are some ways you can cut down the number of meetings you call and not suffer as a result:

Routing schedules. Schedules will serve the purpose of information transfer. Instead of calling everyone together for routine announcements, send the information around for those involved to read at their convenience. Replies can come back to you right on the routing sheet or in separate memos. This works well for exchanging ideas and receiving stimulation and updating.

Idea notebooks. Brainstorming is a helpful exercise, but a time-consuming one. An alternative is a notebook with a statement of a problem that needs solving or a goal you would like to achieve. The notebook should be quite accessible; everyone who wants to should be able to use it as a repository for ideas, thoughts, speculations, and off-the-cuff comments as well as researched propositions. The results of the notebook can be typed up and passed around to everyone working on the project for stimulation and help.

Use conference calls. Part of the increasing time and money cost of meetings is bringing everyone together. Often a face-to-face meeting is unnecessary if everyone involved can be a party to a conference call. (See Chapter 4.)

Use computer conferencing. Even conference calls take up meeting time, although they avoid travel time. Computer conferencing breaks free of real time—you send messages whenever you want to and others will receive them when they check in. This is something like a letter, but much faster, and the computer lets you know the minute your replies come back. Computer conferencing cannot totally replace human contact; you still need that human element for true understanding. But to avoid constant travel or phone interruptions, this is an excellent tool. And when you need an important decision that a number of people should agree on, the computer conference works well. However, if you need to get a decision quickly, the phone is better, since the computer does not communicate urgency effectively.

7.

DELEGATION

Jf you want something done right, you have to do it
yourself." How many times have you heard that old saw and
perhaps even agreed with it? It may be true that doing it
yourself is one way to get things done correctly, but it is also
the most time-consuming way. Do you truly believe that you
must do everything your own way to have it done right?

This do-it-yourself philosophy is one you will have to rid
yourself of if you hope to control your time. Think of it this
way: if you insist on doing everything yourself, your career
and your life will be forever stuck at the level where you *can*
do everything yourself. Furthermore, your subordinates will
become bored, since you refuse to give them anything new or
challenging to do. Before long you may get a reputation as a

poor trainer, or, worse yet, as an easy boss who takes on all the subordinates' work for them.

Here is one way to look at delegation to help you see its merits and importance. Picture yourself as a lever and your subordinates as your fulcrums. The more you use your fulcrums, the greater time advantage you will have. You can leverage time through friends, fellow workers, and outside specialists.

The key to delegation is closeness, which breeds a team spirit. Take the time to learn about your subordinates and show that you care. When you concentrate on the people instead of the work, your delegates will understand that you want them to succeed and do well—rather than simply get the job done by any means. It is important to learn how to delegate, what to delegate, and specific skills that will help you get started with this crucial task. But many managers admit that they do not know how to delegate effectively. Some admit that they fear delegating important jobs, because they are afraid of competition from those who work for them. But learning delegation skills can bring you so many rewards that your fears will seem insignificant once you get started.

Delegation can buy you more working time. It will help you to eliminate, pass on, or at least minimize the time-consuming routine jobs that keep you from your primary work.

Delegation can help you upgrade your subordinates. You do not need to hold formal classroom sessions to teach those who work for you what the department is all about. Rather, give them assignments that will help them develop new skills and abilities. Do this step by step so that you can keep your subordinates challenged but not overwhelmed. Delegation gets training off the theoretical level and into the world of reality by making one cope with a specific assignment. A careful delegation program will mold confident, capable subordinates who will be highly promotable. It will point out those who cannot "cut it" before they rise too far in management.

Delegation multiplies results. If you do it yourself, you can get only so much done. But if you and your entire staff work on a project or problem, the results multiply and expand. And then again, that extra experience will benefit your subordinates.

In today's business climate, it is essential to develop sharp delegation skills. Put the tips in this chapter to work for you now. Here are some reasons why: It is not possible for one manager to keep on top of the market in which he or she must function without help to keep the work flowing. Formerly, most parts of a business could be understood and handled by one person, but now, with computers, complex tax laws, and government regulations, a smart manager allows specialists to handle their areas of expertise, thereby freeing him or her to manage. It is no longer possible in most instances for a boss to expect militarylike responses to his or her commands. Delegation with thorough communication helps employees to understand why they are doing what they are asked to do. Delegation lets managers free themselves from trying to do everything and from not doing anything as well as it should be done. It also allows subordinates to get involved in their managers' jobs, to expand their horizons and try more complex tasks with guidance.

DELEGATION WAYS AND MEANS

The first thing you must do is to determine what needs to be delegated. Routine tasks, for example, even if you could do them quickly yourself, should be delegated so that you need not even think about them anymore.

Ask yourself the following questions when a project comes up: Who else can do this? What would be a better use of my time? When can I start delegating this? How can I do it faster? Why am I the one to do this? The answers will help you determine if you should do the job yourself or delegate it.

You should strive to delegate everything that someone else can do. Keep only the tasks you must do yourself. Things that you believe you do better than others should be delegated, too, especially if they are time-consuming. Teach your subordinates to do them and free yourself for the highest-level work and thinking.

You must also know what not to delegate. Most important, do not delegate work that you do not want to deal with yourself. And do not delegate disciplinary action when this discipline should come from you as department manager. If a subject is confidential, it is imperative that you handle it yourself; otherwise, you risk losing your status as someone who can be confided in by upper management.

If you have several subordinates, it makes sense to set up an assignment chart so that you allocate the work fairly. Such a chart might have spaces to list each person's current assignments, special skills, areas of special education or knowledge, and current time commitments. A chart like this can help you determine the most likely candidate for a project in just a few minutes.

But do not always give the tough jobs to the few most qualified people. When you can, take the time to give your people training jobs in areas they are not familiar with. Encourage your subordinates with special knowledge in these areas to help their peers develop. Show them how such teamwork is rewarded in higher departmental output, and respond positively to those who tutor others when review time comes around.

Get Your Subordinates Involved

Here is what you should cover when you give your subordinates a new assignment:

- *The task*: what it is you want done, in specific terms

- *Considerations*: what you think is important to know as background information for task completion
- *The larger view*: how this task fits into the big picture for the department and the firm
- *Accomplishments*: specifically, what needs to be done to complete this task
- *Responsibility*: both the scope and the limits so that the subordinates know how far they may go within the corporate structure
- *Authority*: necessary so that subordinates will not be too timid or step on toes

Many people say that it is being given responsibility for a job without the authority to get it done properly that is most frustrating. Make sure you set things up for your subordinates with other departments, that they are recognized as your deputies and not as your menials.

Delegate to help others succeed. Do not tell them exactly how to do the job—let them tell you. Exercising their minds will help train them to do their own work in the future. Share information, background material, and considerations with them, but let them shape the form the project will take—but be available to answer questions, of course.

If the task you are delegating is new, you do not have to assign the whole job at once. Try outlining the entire project and asking your delegate to report when the first step has been completed. Then you can evaluate the actions to date and proceed with the next step.

It is up to you to make sure that the reports you ask for are delivered on time if your delegate does not volunteer them. Make sure that your people know that you do keep track of what they have been assigned and that the jobs are not just busy work.

And make sure you and your delegate take time to evaluate

the work on a job once it has been completed. This should be a private affair, especially if you must criticize the subordinate's work. If praise is in order, that can be given in public as well as on a one-to-one basis.

The Nuts and Bolts of Delegation

Here are some how-to tips to help you get started practicing this exceptional time-saving art:

Practice delegation. You are going to have to get comfortable with the art of delegation; until you do, you will find it easier to do the work yourself than to delegate it. Begin to practice by refusing to get directly involved with a project. Keep pushing your delegate to do it. If he or she tries to pass it off to you, stay aloof and merely give advice and pointers. Do not let that file folder or notebook land on your desk until the project is through. Be firm.

Use a delegation file. In addition to the chart of subordinates that lists their current projects and areas of expertise, make sure you keep an up-to-date delegation file detailing the assignments you give to each person. Put the scheduled reporting dates in this file and on your calendar. If you do not postpone the reports, subordinates will get the idea that you mean business.

Take time to teach a task. How many times have you put off delegating a duty because it has to be taught to your assistant? Take the time once to teach that skill, and you will be free of that task for good.

Listen well. After you have given the assignment clearly and explained reporting methods and times, listen carefully to what your subordinate says. It is up to you to act as an early warning device to head off problems. Watch for uncertainty about schedules, discomfort in discussions, fuzzy data, delays without basis. Investigate while the problem is still of manageable size.

Make sure that you are understood. Here is what a machinery company vice-president says about delegation communications: "I find miscommunication is the biggest time-waster of them all. If I give an assignment, for example, and there is miscommunication, all the time spent doing it is wasted, plus the time to correct it or recommunicate the assignment and have it done again. Also, subtle misunderstandings rob time from every day. Now I take the time to be sure I'm understood correctly the first time, even if I have to go over and over and over again until we get it right. In the long run, that's the shortest route to speedy communications."

Do not solve delegates' problems for them. Too often, your delegate will come to you with a question, and you will end up working out the whole project. You have lost the time-saving advantage of delegation, and they have lost the opportunity to discover a personal solution. Insist that when your delegates have problems to discuss with you, they come armed with some possible solutions of their own. Then you can help them choose the best one and send them off to implement it themselves.

Test your delegates' readiness. If you doubt whether a certain subordinate is ready to take on a certain job, play a "what if" game and see. Identify two or three central areas of knowledge crucial to seeing the project through. Ask your delegate, "What would you do if one of these areas started causing problems?" The answer will tell you how knowledgeable your delegate is in this area and how well he or she can handle the inevitable close calls.

The best test comes while you are away. Next time you need to go out of town, test your subordinates' newfound skills. Delegate some assignments you might have handled if you were in town, and see how your delegates do in your absence. How well are routine activities carried on without you, and which seem to need you around for guidance or watchdog duty?

Use meetings to serve two delegation purposes. Send a delegate to some of the meetings you usually attend yourself. This will, first, save you the time of attending. Second, it will expose your subordinate to some new activities and decision-making processes. Ask your delegate to write a concise report on the meeting (ten minutes maximum reading or hearing time). It will be challenging for the delegate to distill the important parts of the meeting for you, and you will get an edited report that will serve you almost as well as personal attendance in a fraction of the time.

8.

OFFICE INTERACTION

As a manager, you may well have a few, or even a few hundred, subordinates reporting to you, in addition to a secretary or assistant. You must build your staff into a competent management team to increase staff productivity, to work well with your subordinates without allowing them to tyrannize you or vice versa, and to organize projects so that you and your team meet reasonable deadlines with grace and effectiveness.

Robert Half, a Philadelphia-based consultant, says that time loss within American organizations represents a monetary loss of more than $100 billion a year. Because of this enormous time-and-money drain, you owe it to your firm to encourage your staff to take time management seriously, just as you do. Here are some ways to form a time-effective team and work well together.

DEVELOP A MANAGEMENT TEAM

A whole football team can move the ball toward the goal much more effectively than any one or two players working alone. By the same token, a well-chosen and well-developed management team can accomplish things that the team's manager could never do, working as an individual.

With the proper planning and staffing, a management team can direct and guide current activities, forecast and plan for future programs, explore and develop new ideas or ventures, and use every available resource. A four-step process—recruiting, training, development, and utilization—helps you develop such a team for whatever purpose you determine. Results take time, but in most cases they are well worth nurturing.

Recruiting

Most of the team members you need may already be on your staff, but do not assume so. Evaluate your people on the basis of managerial strengths and weaknesses. To do this, you might use charts with columns showing their education, training, financial background, marketing background, or engineering background.

If you find you are too heavy in marketing and too light in finance, for example, keep this in mind when it comes time to add staff. Recruit new managers with the thought of building a more well-rounded team. In other words, do not start firing or laying off good people just because their specialties are too much alike, but when vacancies occur, hire new managers with strengths that your department could use. Transfers or promotions from other departments of the firm could help as well, especially since these employees would already have some experience with your firm and its quirks.

Training

Make sure that your people have an overall view of your business. Do not keep them cloistered in their own area of specialty; give them assignments that will make them interact with other departments to learn and teach. Let your own team members work together so that marketing pros start catching on to what data processing is all about, and so forth. This you-teach-me, I'll-teach-you concept does not have to be rigidly enforced. The smart managers on your team will automatically take advantage of the opportunity to learn from others, and they are the ones who will become your team leaders of the future.

Development

Foster team spirit and team interaction. Put the team members' offices in close proximity. Assign them to a variety of projects in different combinations. Have regular team meetings to discuss progress on these projects.

Team members should share responsibility for each project. No one designated leader should shoulder the burden for everything. Rewards should come from decisions arrived at through a consensus; individual actions and approaches should be saved for a more appropriate setting.

Group trips to conferences and conventions may help to build good feeling among team members. Group-think sessions can be helpful as well, as can social occasions to celebrate successes and changes brought about by the team.

Do not do all this without revealing your motivations; it is helpful to explain to your subordinates that you are trying to build a team with their help.

Utilization

Once your management team is shaping up, identify a major project or two for the team to tackle. Explain the project, then get their input, advice, and support. Make sure the team has as much responsibility and authority as possible to deal with its particular problem area.

A valuable project—in addition to more immediate ones you may assign—is to have the team do a three- to six-year plan for the firm or the department. Several alternate paths can be explored, along with contingency plans and utilization outlines for manpower, equipment, and capital.

INCREASE PRODUCTIVITY IN YOUR DEPARTMENT

Productivity is slipping in American business. According to O. Mark Marcussen, a management consultant with Theodore Barry and Associates, the greatest slip in productivity has occurred in the executive suite rather than on the production line. Marcussen has done studies which show that 3.6 hours out of the 8-hour workday are wasted. Even allowing 1.2 hours for personal time, this means that 2.4 hours go totally down the drain each day.

Such waste is a management concern and a management problem. Solutions exist, however, that can cut that wasted time and increase employee output as much as 25 percent.

Define Tasks

Your first step in increasing productivity is to define the tasks that need to be done and document the steps that move the job to completion. You may well find that a number of people are doing jobs that overlap in one or more areas.

This documentation may show up some pointless work done on one level and passed on to another level that has no real use. And in discussing the key tasks with your subordinates, it may come out that they have different goals and expectations than you do. Such discussions are especially valuable if you can pinpoint things that are done because "we've always done it that way" or because "that's how I was taught to do it" way back when. Examine these seeming "must" jobs to find which are needed tasks and which have been kept through inertia.

Determine the Time Scope

When you have a thinned-out list of necessary tasks, you will need to find out how long it takes to perform each task, how many people are needed to complete it, and what resources are necessary for the job. Do not just look up the historical data on these jobs; get a fresh look at the process to help you pinpoint areas of waste. To do this, discuss the time scope issue with your subordinates, find out how much time they are spending, and get their input as to which parts of the task seem unnecessary, overdocumented, or whatever. Discover where streamlining can take place to cut the time allocated for each job.

Training for Work-Flow Control

One of the biggest time drains occurs when capable people have nothing to do even though they have asked their manager for more work. Making a tight schedule, assigning work with care, and coordinating activities so that everyone has a fair load of work at all times is quite an assignment for any manager. There will always be some drain in this area; you cannot schedule perfectly. But you can make sure there are back-up tasks for those temporarily out of something to do, and you can check to see that jobs are not overstaffed. You should make sure that your people have a clear understanding of what management expects of them so that they do not hide in a corner when they have finished the visible work assigned to them.

DEALING WITH SECRETARIES AND ASSISTANTS

Your subordinates can be your greatest allies in improving your time use if they are trained to help you. As the boss, you may be able to lighten the load for your direct employees by clearing out unnecessary and repetitive clerical work and freeing the secretary or assistant to take on more interesting and stimulating work.

Is Your Secretary as Helpful as Possible?

How do you utilize your secretary? Does he or she do all of the tasks that could be handled from his or her desk? The National Secretaries Association (2440 Pershing Road, Kansas City, Missouri 64108) has created a prototypical secretarial job description. Look over this description with your secretary, and see if he or she is doing everything covered that applies to your business. If not, discuss training and outside seminars that could help boost your secretary's skills. Perhaps your secretary should begin working on the Certified Professional Secretary (CPS) program sponsored by the National Secretaries Association (NSA). (Complete information is available from them at the address above.) According to the NSA, a secretary does the following:

- Relieves the executive of various administrative details
- Coordinates and maintains effective office procedures and efficient work flow

- Implements policies and procedures set by the employer
- Establishes and maintains harmonious working relationships with superiors, co-workers, subordinates, customers or clients, and suppliers
- Schedules appointments and maintains the calendar
- Receives and assists visitors and telephone callers and refers them to executives or other appropriate persons as circumstances warrant
- Arranges business itineraries and coordinates the executive's travel requirements
- Takes action authorized during the executive's absence and uses initiative and judgment to see that matters requiring attention are referred to delegated authority or handled in a manner to minimize effect of the employer's absence
- Takes manual shorthand and transcribes from it or transcribes from machine dictation
- Types material from longhand or rough copy
- Sorts, reads, and annotates incoming mail and documents and attaches the appropriate file to facilitate necessary action
- Determines routing, signatures required, and maintains follow-up
- Composes correspondence and reports for own or executive's signature
- Prepares communication outlined by the executive in oral or written directions
- Researches and abstracts information and supporting data in preparation for meetings, work projects, and reports
- Correlates and edits materials submitted by others
- Organizes material that may be presented to the executive in draft form

- Maintains the filing and a records management system and other office-flow procedures
- Makes arrangements for and coordinates conferences and meetings, serving, if necessary, as a recorder of minutes with responsibility for transcription and distribution to participants
- May supervise or hire other employees; select and/or make recommendations for purchase of supplies and equipment; maintain budget and expense account records, financial reports, and confidential files
- Maintains an up-to-date procedures manual for the specific duties handled on the job
- Performs other duties as assigned or as judgment or necessity dictates

Training Your Own Executive Assistant

Administrative assistants are cropping up all over these days, but many managers are not so sure what they should be doing or how training should take place. This position is somewhat different from that of a secretary: the administrative assistant is truly an executive assistant with special knowledge of the business and the authority to take some steps toward solutions, changes, and the like independently.

One of the best ways for you to get more done without working longer hours is to have such high-level help in your office. But in order to get such help you may have to do the training yourself. Assuming you can select a person you like and trust, here is a suggested training program that will help you get your assistant ready for the action.

INITIAL TRAINING

For the first several days your assistant should act as an observer, following you to see how you operate, what jobs you do, with whom you communicate. Within the limits of your time schedule, try to answer questions as they come up. And make a special effort to look at your job from this novice's point of view; do not assume knowledge your assistant has no way of having. Explain fully—emphasizing important concepts and important people—the keys to your position.

When your assistant seems to have a fairly good orientation, start giving assignments and responsibilities. But do not make these general assignments like "sort the mail" or "pick up the reports in the other departments." Starting assistants off on a superficial level is a typical mistake many managers make.

Your assistant will get off to a much better start if you give him or her vertical knowledge rather than horizontal, superficial knowledge at the start. (Vertical knowledge includes all aspects of a job, from start to finish. Horizontal knowledge implies limitation to a certain area.) In other words, choose one or two serious projects and turn over complete control to your assistant. Let your assistant act as a fully involved, responsible member of the management team.

Having a full project instead of dribs and drabs of your projects will feed your assistant's ego and build confidence. And you will be able to size up this person's overall readiness and areas of strength and weakness in an actual business situation.

Do not abandon your assistant, however. Ask him or her to do all the legwork, fact-gathering, and compiling and to work on some alternate plans of attack. Then formulate solutions and discuss options.

MIDDLE TRAINING PERIOD

As your assistant becomes acclimated and completes a few projects with your supervision, take a further step and delegate certain responsibilities on a more or less permanent basis. Here are some ideas on what this delegation might entail:

Daily scheduling. Having your assistant work up your To Do Today sheet will free you from this task and help him or her get a grasp of the overall responsibilities of the department. But make sure you have your assistant leave you at least 20 percent discretionary time so that you do not become hemmed in and overly dependent upon the schedule.

Routine correspondence. Perhaps your secretary already does this for you, but if not, it might be the best way to get your assistant involved in all aspects of your responsibility. For a while, check your assistant's outgoing letters before they leave the department. Once you are confident that he or she can handle the greatest percentage of correspondence effectively, do not bother checking any longer. Trust your assistant to ask you for help if a knotty problem develops.

Researching and interviewing. This one will be a big time-saver for you, but it is a responsibility some executives are fearful of giving up. Whenever you have a question that needs research or information from someone in another department, have your assistant get the information. Give him or her some pointers on where to find the facts you need, but do not give away a step-by-step plan. That will lower the assignment to the busy-work realm. Meanwhile, you will be free to work on something that only you can do effectively.

Assignments for the Fully Trained Assistant

As time goes on, your assistant may well be able to become your true surrogate in a number of situations. For example, your assistant can go to meetings for you, give a report for you, or get some questions answered.

Have your assistant take over some of your reading. Better than anyone else, your trained assistant knows what you look for in trade publications, books, and reports. Let him or her search for this specific information, point it out to you, and thereby save you that hunting time for more pressing jobs. In addition, this exposure to literature in your field will provide a goldmine of learning for your subordinate.

Ask your assistant for solutions and not just problems. Whenever your assistant approaches you about a problem, he or she should come equipped with possible solutions. This is good training for your assistant, and it frees you from doing the preliminary head work on the problem. You can help your assistant select the right solution. And even if he or she does not have the best solution, the assistant's groundwork will help you come to the proper decision more quickly.

Give the assistant authority over specific things such as hiring, firing, assignments to other subordinates, your schedule, and travel. Such assignments free you for your top-priority work, and you should feed them to your assistant as soon as he or she is capable of handling them.

Rules for a Good Working Relationship

Get certain rules and regulations straight between you and your assistant or secretary. Such a discussion will avoid miscommunication that can waste time and foster hard feelings. Here are some of the regulations you might consider:

Set a time to report. Your assistant needs to know that there will be a definite time for reporting the status of current projects and for receiving new work assignments. Set a definite time each day. That way, you will avoid having him or her interrupt you. Make sure you stick to the reporting time, too; do not interrupt your assistant unless it is really necessary. Also, have your assistant report to you by short, written notes— for example, "Smith file complete" or "All reservations confirmed for Dallas trip." Or have your assistant report only when results or actions differ from the plan agreed upon. This requires that you trust your assistant to handle things correctly.

Categorize jobs. Have an understanding with your secretary or assistant as to what words such as *urgent* and *rush* mean.

Make sure your gradations of priority are straight. Here are some possible definitions:

- Urgent: must be done immediately
- Rush: complete within 24 hours
- Priority: need within one week
- Future: complete as time allows

You can use a printed form on a job as you assign it, and check the category that applies.

Keep your assistant fully informed. When you explain the ins and outs of your business to your assistant, you prepare him or her to handle decision-making tasks for you. Your assistant will know that you trust him or her with the information, and that you respect your assistant's capacity to use that information. Make sure your helper is aware of what is important, who is important, what the major departmental goals are, and how they should be achieved. Soon you will find that he or she can independently handle more calls and replies than before and free you for other business.

Let your assistant or secretary learn the inside structure. You should learn this structure of your firm and share your knowledge of it with your assistant. For instance, who gives out purchase order numbers, and who does it when he or she is out? What are the key information centers that supply you with facts for your monthly reports and planning sessions? Keep notes on these very important people, and be alert to changing casts of characters as responsibilities are delegated or people leave. And always share your knowledge of these changes with your assistant so that he or she can gather information for you swiftly.

Seek common goals. If you are aiming to improve the level of production, say, even if quality control suffers a bit, and your assistant is working to improve quality control at all costs, you may be working at cross purposes. You need rules about what is important to the department and to you as individuals. Such goals could also include upgradings in performance by your assistant, with mutually agreed upon rewards like salary increases, fringe benefits, or promotions. Just make sure you can deliver on your promises when your assistant or secretary meets the goals you have set together.

Make sure that your subordinates understand what you expect from them. Expect your subordinates to improve their own time management. Make this an ongoing expectation, not something you push for a month or so and allow to drop from the scene. Expect subordinates to do their best and to perform at a consistently high level. Be specific about what this means to you in terms of results. Knowing exactly what goals you have in mind for them will help your people meet those goals; they will not waste time and energy trying to figure it out for themselves. Expect the best, not the worst from people. If you expect your people to learn from their mistakes, they are more likely to do so. If you expect these people to improve their time use, express that expectation, and you are more than likely to see such an improvement.

Do not make your subordinates wait for you. Start your meetings on time. Do not keep people on hold minute after minute—respect others' time and they will respect yours.

Do not keep subordinates popping in and out of your office. It is not necessary to call them in for every little item that occurs to you. Try to handle all assignments and discussions in a scheduled reporting period once a day or several times a week. This gives your subordinates the freedom to schedule their own days without fear of tyranny from you.

Do not interrupt subordinates. Just as you do not like to be interrupted, you should avoid running into their offices at will, since it disrupts their plans for the day and makes them nervous.

Do not keep piling assignment upon assignment. Some managers keep adding work until their subordinates holler.

The trouble is that some people will keep accepting that work and toil past the point of exhaustion. Others will reject the work, but keep secret the fact that it is not being done. It is up to you as the boss to calculate a fair amount of work for each of your subordinates so that they are busy but not overburdened.

Make subordinates think about what they do. You may jostle their minds enough to improve their time use. Be bold every once in a while and ask, "Why are you wasting your time on that?" Your challenge will force them to explain why the job is worth doing. And if they cannot think of reasons for doing it, it probably is a waste of time and a task that should be dropped anyway.

Step aside from bottlenecks. Sometimes, you are the one who is blind to the best answer. If you are stymied by a tough decision or an unsolvable problem, get others' ideas, and implement one of their suggestions or solutions. But remember not to burst in on your people when the problem comes to light; present it at their regular reporting time, or call a special meeting that fits into both of your schedules.

Avoid promoting to incompetence. One widespread problem among organizations large and small is the "reward concept" of promotion to management. In other words, the top-producing salesman is "rewarded" with the job of sales manager; the best machine operator gets a shot at the foreman's post. But what happens to that top person when he or she starts that new job totally untrained in the effective use of human resources? If your firm promotes people on the reward basis, at least make sure that part of the reward is proper training: exposure to time-management and people-management concepts and practice, and a mentor that the new manager can consult for advice and help.

Get time-saving tips from your staff. Suggestion-box systems work. They yield new ideas and improve staff morale, so implement a time-saving suggestion box to yield specific ideas from your staff. A research organization devoted to the study of suggestion systems says that for every dollar you spend on programs soliciting employee suggestions, you should receive an average of thirty dollars' worth of practicable ideas.

Offer monetary rewards. (A recent average reward is $111 for an idea put successfully into practice.) You may wish to compensate the idea-giver on a scale that varies according to the long-term value of his or her idea. Do not expect 100 percent participation. Studies show that you will involve about one in five of your employees. Of the suggestions received, about a third will be practicable. Be sure to get the legal rights to the ideas. Once your employee receives a reward, you should have him or her sign over all legal rights to the idea to avoid later conflicts.

Do not overmanage. A study made in England points up the importance of allowing workers to feel involved in their work and related decisions. Three groups were tested: one managed in the traditional, tightly controlled way; one with employees free to make suggestions and choose their own break times; and one that operated without rules or soliciting advice of any kind. The anarchical team was twice as profitable as the participatory team and ten times as profitable as the tightly controlled team.

Use friendly rivalry. A bit of rivalry can encourage better productivity in your subordinates. If you give complementary portions of a project to rival employees, they will compete to see who can outshine the other, so that you get a better product from each of them. Another technique is to give projects of a similar nature to two rivals and let them know you will be watching to see how effective their solutions are.

Here are a few pointers to help you keep the rivalry productive and not let it degenerate into a free-for-all: (1) Judge the rivals against their own previous performances, not just against each other. (2) Reward everyone who turns in fine work, not just the person who did the superior job. (3) Vary the types of jobs and assignments you give rivals so that each has his or her own chance to shine. Do not let the rivalry become one-sided, or you will defeat your purpose; the winner will have it too easy, and the loser may become demoralized. (4) Do not allow a killer attitude to develop; if things are becoming too cut-throat, step back from the rivalry technique for a time.

Make sure your subordinates know the value of your time. The production manager of a fabricating company gave us this hint:

> I knew the value of my time, but my subordinates obviously did not. And their ineffectiveness hampered my output. To get them to speed up, I learned how to motivate effectiveness in others: (1) I pointed out personal rewards they could earn; (2) I tied greater output directly to time off, promotion, or some other desirable goal; (3) I preempted fears of rush-rush pressure with hard information on time-management techniques. The plan worked and my people now help each other to improve their total productivity.

Keep your relationships cordial. If you detect ill will on the part of your secretary or assistant or if you simply want to make sure such bad feelings never develop, a list of facilitating conditions from the *Secretary* magazine should help you test yourself and your department. Here are some factors, according to Alma Baron, that create a positive working atmosphere:

- An understanding by your secretary or assistant of your expectations
- Discussion of mutual goals and objectives on a regular basis
- Use of good judgment by both parties
- Respect for himself or herself and for the other
- Open communication both ways
- Understanding of the executive's job on the part of

the secretary, with the executive explaining the reasons for what is done
- Loyalty and integrity, flowing both ways
- High motivation to work well together, by mutual agreement
- Maturity in interpersonal relationships

Encourage your secretary or assistant to be assertive in stating his or her needs, and be open to discuss these needs as well as your own. When you sense a problem, treat it immediately by discussing it and finding a solution; do not allow it to fester.

Increasing Efficiency of Assistants

Turning from the broad issue of relationships, consider some nuts-and-bolts ideas designed to foster better communications and understanding, as well as to save time for you and upgrade the quality of your assistant's job functions.

Taking phone messages. Encourage your secretary or assistant to take better phone messages. Expect as much information as possible from the caller so that the call can be handled without your getting involved. If you must return the call, expect your assistant to provide necessary files and other support material along with the message.

Blocking interruptions. Your secretary or assistant should serve as "information gate-keeper" to allow you that all-important quiet hour each day. Even when you are seeing people, your secretary or assistant should screen all visitors to make sure their quest is one that must be handled directly by you.

Try using a "job jar." A popular comic strip features a job jar from which the husband pulls one slip of paper each time he has a day off. Each slip contains a household chore his wife wants him to do. Try this technique at the office for some of those jobs that never seem to get done—filing competitive samples, organizing drawers for greater efficiency, and so on.

When your assistant has a bit of free time and energy, suggest that he or she draw a job from the jar. The luck of the draw adds a bit of excitement to the concept of catching up on overdue support work.

Word processing. The word-processing department is lauded by some as a time saver that cuts routine letter writing and improves typist efficiency. Others fear it will destroy the relationship between executive and secretary. Before starting a word-processing department, be sure the level of your routine and standard correspondence warrants the purchase of this expensive editing equipment. And do not let the processing equipment become a substitute for personal secretaries; executives need organizational skills, shielding from outside distractions, and good filing as much as they need dictation and typing help.

Use different colored marking pens for different instructions. Use red for "things to do," green for "please type this up," blue for "route this to," purple for "file under," and so forth. This saves writing or giving the same instructions hundreds of times.

Use part-time help to avoid overtime. When your work activity level rises for a short period of time, your first instinct may be to ask your secretary or assistant to work overtime. If he or she is on a career track headed for advancement toward an executive position, this request may be met with a very positive response as an opportunity to prove devotion and competence. But people who plan to remain clerical workers often meet the idea of overtime with reluctance. If this is the case in your operation, why not take the same money you would use to pay overtime and hire a part-time or temporary clerical worker. Let your regular help delegate the jobs to the temporary person so that you do not need to get involved. Your staff won't be overburdened by overtime.

Streamlining ideas. If you look over the work that your secretary or assistant normally turns out, you will most probably find that a great deal of it consists of paperwork—letters, memos, and routine reports. There are three ways to cut down on this endless stream of time-consuming paper:

First, use "speed memos." Write your answer on the letter or note that comes to you instead of composing a full-fledged letter for a short answer. All your secretary will have to do is get the answer into an envelope after copying the original letter and your reply on the photocopier.

Second, use phone calls for simple yes or no answers and a short handwritten memo for answers to simple questions. The formality of a full memo or letter is not called for on most everyday questions.

Third, use graphs, summaries, and outlines instead of long reports full of verbiage. Facts and figures in a terse, easy-to-grasp form will please the recipients as well.

Give your secretary or assistant some variety. To keep your well-trained helpers on your payroll, do not let them succumb to the mental fatigue that may send them to the "help wanted" section. Give your people a variety of assignments, including plenty of new challenges and learning experiences. Do not save all the plum assignments for yourself if your assistant or secretary can handle them. From time to time shift your people from assignment to assignment. Or at the very least, vary what your people do from morning to afternoon and from day to day.

Evaluating Performance

Make sure you have a way of evaluating what is taking place in your department when the improved productivity work-flow system is in effect. Such an ongoing evaluation will help you know where to modify reporting relationships, task definitions and standards, and the like. Willingness and ability to change to meet various circumstances are important in maintaining a smooth work flow. As productivity increases and the flow of work becomes smooth and more predictable, managers and workers will applaud the new system. That boost in productivity—up to 25 percent—should lead to favorable reviews and salary increases in the long run.

Avoiding Tyranny by Subordinates

Subordinates are there to help you, right? You delegate to them and they take work off your hands, in theory at least. But how much time do you spend doing—or fixing—your subordinate's work? One study shows that the average manager spends up to a fourth of his or her time doing or redoing work that should have been completed by subordinates.

This does not necessarily mean that your subordinates are plotting to turn their work back to you; actually, they do it naturally. Many subordinates fear making decisions or even presenting alternatives; they would prefer to be led by the hand. Their docile behavior can consume your time if you let it. But a better strategy is to learn how to get that work back in your subordinate's court so that you will be free to do the work you should be doing. Here are some of the subordinate's gambits and how to avoid them:

"We've got a problem." Your subordinate has a problem. Since you are the boss, he or she thinks that it should be your problem, too. Your subordinate comes to you and outlines the problem and asks you to handle it or otherwise leaves it squarely in your lap.

Without thinking, you may start to give the person some ideas on how to handle your common problem. If the problem is more complex than that, you may suggest that he or she leave the relevant materials with you so that you can think it over. That way, the subordinate leaves your office whistling, free of the problem until further notice. You are weighted down with yet another thing to worry about.

"When can I have your approval." This is another ploy subordinates use to get the monkey off their own back and onto yours. They may hand you a memo or a file on the situation at hand. Then they will say, "I'll leave this with you for your approval." They drop the information like a hot potato and leave you with the problem.

"Let's get together to talk about this." Another variation on the above. The subordinate wants to delay the project, so he or she comes up with a stumbling block that requires your advice. All your subordinate has to do is to spend a few minutes reviewing the project, until he or she comes up with a problem that could require your help. This rough assessment is all that gets done on the project until you come to the rescue.

"Only you can handle it." Watch out for this ploy. It is designed to feed your ego. Your subordinate may even try a line like "You do this so much better than I do." And you may well fall for it.

If you have been falling for these ploys, ask yourself what you need all these helpers for if their main function is to shuffle work back up to you. You do need them, to free you for work that is your own exclusive challenge. So start defending yourself and helping your subordinates to spread their own wings as managers. Here is how:

Do not let your subordinates give you work. If your subordinates discover a problem, require them to make an appointment with you to discuss it—no dropping in with random queries. You may see your subordinates in person or have a phone discussion. Do not encourage them to write you a memo, because then you must write back. A discussion will take less time and allow for quicker communication of ideas.

Make sure your subordinates do the work you assign. Do not end up doing it yourself, no matter what. You may advise, consult, support, encourage, channel, and coordinate the work, but the subordinates should do the contacting, thinking, planning, and doing. If the first subordinate to whom the work is assigned simply cannot handle it, reassign the work to another subordinate.

Make a specific time limit for dealing with subordinates. Your subordinates will devour your time if you allow it, so draw your own arbitrary time limit for each week.

Make specific assignments, with deadlines. Do not simply tell them to "think about the assignment." Since there is no concrete proof of thinking, you will have no way to evaluate the efforts put forth. As an alternative, why not have them think about a problem and bring you several alternate solutions by a certain date.

Keep the ball in the other guy's court. It is natural for your subordinates to pass work along to you; you may be able to relate to it in terms of your relationship with your own boss. But if you return all their serves and lobs into your court, you can defend yourself against the time drain of doing the subordinates' work.

Time-wasters and Trouble-makers

There is no reason why some people on your staff should be allowed to be chronic time-wasters, whose lazy habits cut into the effectiveness of everyone around. The *Wall Street Transcript* suggests ways to "psych out" the reasons why your time-wasters do waste time and ways to help the offenders break the nasty habit. Here are some symptoms you may encounter:

Boredom. Someone who complains and has a hangdog look may be searching for a challenge. Give this person a larger work load with some juicy projects.

Too many ideas. Some characters have an idea a minute and have to share them with you and everyone else within earshot. Try explaining to this person that ideas should be put down on paper for you to review. In this way, you can separate the wheat from the chaff without being interrupted. Or to avoid paperwork, you might suggest that the ideas be made a part of this person's regular reporting time with you.

Lack of confidence. Some employees dillydally because they are afraid to take a stand and complete a job that may be criticized. Offer praise and encouragement. A better self-image is the key here.

Excess of confidence. Enthusiastic ego-plus workers think the world is waiting for their input any time they feel ready to give it. Again, insist that their comments be put on paper in the form of structured reports to avoid wasting time.

Thoughtlessness. The slob, the jester, and the gossip are less apt to react to the kid-gloves treatment. They need firm reprimands and ultimatums. You may need to resort to such strong tactics with the other types listed as well if your psychological treatment does not yield improvement.

Another type of time-waster is the office troublemaker. Most office workers are reasonably easy to deal with, but about 10 percent are truly difficult, according to management consultant Robert M. Bramson. Here are some typical troublemaker types and a few hints on dealing with them:

Hostile-aggressives can be "Sherman tanks," "snipers," or "exploders." The key thing is not to take their bait—to remain cool. Stand up to the person, but do not get into a fight. Let him or her blow off steam. If all else fails, say you are leaving the room and will return in five minutes. This allows the hostile-aggressive worker time to collect his or her wits.

Complainers exaggerate their woes and expect long-suffering sympathy. Do not agree or disagree—just feed back noncommittal "uh-huhs."

Indecisives can be "analysts" or "be-nicers" who fear making enemies. You can help the analyst by giving him or her evidence and reinforcing its facts-and-figures basis. With be-nicers, find out what the real meaning of the indecisiveness is. Give the person a deadline to make a decision and then leave, saying that you will be back for the answer at deadline time.

Unresponsives are afraid. Let them know you are friendly and nonthreatening and wait them out until they are ready to talk.

Know-it-alls can be "really right" people who know a lot or they can be "phony experts." Meet the know-it-all with your own facts and figures in line. He or she can be convinced by logic and evidence.

In summary, managing your own behavior can help you deal with difficult personalities without wasting undue amounts of time. Underlying all this is the assumption that the troublemaker has enough going for him or her to be kept on the staff. Unless you are the boss, you may be forced to deal with the troublemakers whom your boss finds helpful—but these methods can be used in this circumstance, too.

DEALING WITH SUPERIORS

The previous sections outline techniques that you can use when you are in control—when you are the boss who can dictate how things are to be done, when you can be interrupted, how projects are to be organized and assigned, and so on. Now our focus is on situations when you cannot lay down the law, when you are the subordinate.

Unfortunately, there is no 100 percent effective way to make your boss understand the importance of time management and your commitment to it. That is one reason why we advise never to schedule your day without a margin for unexpected interruptions or changes in plans. But there are some things you can do to let people know that you try to get full use out of your time; perhaps you can even interest them in doing the same.

If your schedule is often blown because of last-minute projects your boss throws at you or his or her frequent pop-in visits, here are some techniques you can try to reduce the interruptions:

Educate your boss. Refer to your own efforts to organize your time and what these efforts have done to improve department performance. Make tactful occasional suggestions when you see a way your boss might improve his or her time use. Let your boss know of your progress in time-management skills—for example, improved concentration span, quiet-hour implementation, a set of goals developed, and a step-by-step program under way. When it is time to give your boss a gift for a holiday, birthday, or whatever, you might give a good time-management book or a newsletter subscription to *Execu-Time*. (For a sample copy of *Execu-Time* and a free copy of the booklet *166 Effective Time-Saving Tips for Executives,* write *Execu-Time* at the address on page 60.)

Keep your priority and To Do Today lists visible. When your boss tosses a new hot potato to you, pull out your priority list and go over it together. You have the right to ask how your boss wants you to reorder the work; you should not be obligated to squeeze it all in as if the new assignment were just an additional job to be completed in the same time frame, assuming that you have a full schedule already.

Ask how long the job should take. Each time you receive an assignment from your boss, inquire as to how long he or she expects it should take you to complete it. Keep careful records on how long the job actually takes, with your best efforts to complete it promptly and well. Include the time information with your final report on the job. If your boss has been underestimating the time it takes to do the jobs he or she gives you, this should help improve the estimates.

Admit your limitations. Some bosses—especially those on the "fast track"—think that you can do anything. They think that you should be willing to pile on assignment after assignment, increasing your workweek to fifty, sixty, or even seventy hours.

Perhaps for a very important short-term project this can be done, but as a steady diet it is unhealthy and unfair. If all else fails with your boss, it is up to you to declare your human limitations. Be honest about what you can and cannot accomplish by the deadline, allowing yourself time for proper sleep and recreation. You owe it to yourself to do this: some bosses expect it. They say that they gauge when to stop piling on the work by when the employee hollers uncle.

Learn to cope with waiting. Here is a tip from the purchasing director of a metal-working company on what to do when your boss or a visitor keeps you waiting for an appointment:

> I was bugged by people who never showed, or who showed up late, for appointments with me. I'd stop work and be sitting for ten, fifteen, twenty minutes or longer. I finally decided I couldn't afford the wasted time, so now I do a few things to minimize the loss. First, I keep right on working as though the appointment does not exist; this eliminates my stopping work early and idly waiting. Second, I always have some quick reading material at hand, or other short pieces of work I can pick up and put down at a moment's notice. Then, when I do finish up a meeting or other large piece of work in time for an appointment, I can keep busy until the other person actually shows up.
>
> Finally, I observe the general rule: "The person who wants more from the other should be the pursuer." This means, if I want something from someone else, I'll call, write, and otherwise pursue it to make sure the appointment happens as scheduled. But if the other guy wants something from me, then I'll sit tight and keep working, and wait for him to make contact with me.

Another schedule squelcher is the boss who calls a meeting for 2:00 P.M. and shows up minutes or even hours late. To save your sanity and your schedule, try taking some portable work with you to the meeting or, if possible, right into the room where the boss is. That way, he or she will see how unperturbed you are over the wait, that you can get things done in any setting. A second alternative is to wait a short time and do a few short tasks. Then tell your superior's secretary that you will be available in your office and ask to be called when the meeting is ready to start.

DEALING WITH PEERS

Here are some techniques that can keep you from losing too much time to peers' demands, without seeming rude or overly terse.

Learn to say no. A chief executive officer in a large agricultural organization gives this idea for saying no to demands on his time that he cannot handle: "My first level turndown is: 'I'm sorry, but I don't have the five (or whatever number) of hours I would need *to do your project justice.*' If that doesn't work, I come back with: 'I'll do what you ask if you do something for me in return.' Then I make a comparable request for my caller's time and effort. I've had only *one* person accept. The rest of the time, I'm home free."

Get financial data in an accessible form. Are you spending too much time figuring out the financial data your accounting department feeds to you? Accountants who are not familiar with time-management principles are likely to supply their reports in a lengthy format that is hard to digest quickly. Why not ask your finance people to provide you with an overview in chart form or to pull out the specific numbers and facts that you need on a flash report to accompany the long back-up piece they supply.

Use printouts efficiently. We have seen many executives struggling with 100-page printouts that slide off the desk and roll out like Slinky toys as the pages unfurl. Are those fat printouts you get filled with useful, up-to-date information? Or are you paging through outdated material to get to the live printout?

Invest a little time with your data-processing people to help them trim the fat from that printout, and you will save time paging through the report. Remember that printout paper is expensive. Do save one of the fat reports for the archives, just in case.

Forget the rumor mill. Do not waste any time gossiping or listening to gossip. You will find out the truth soon enough, and worrying about who is getting ahead can keep you from working on the project that will get you ahead.

Broadcast your commitment to time management. Let everyone know your commitment to good time use. It is a good example for them, and it puts a healthy pressure on you to manage your time effectively. If you do not, someone will notice and comment, and the criticism will get you back on track to make the next deadline or cut that wasteful activity.

9.

PAPERWORK

The best way to evaluate the reams of paper that cross your desk is to cost them out. Figure the cost of your time for handling the paperwork; for writing and editing it if it is your own creation; and for all the people who gather facts, prepare them, process them, and present them to you. Then try to decide how much it costs those who receive your correspondence and reports to read and use what you have sent out.

Chances are you will not be able to get a concrete figure, because of all the direct and indirect costs that will occur to you when you begin trying to get a handle on your paperwork investment. But count up as high as you can before abandoning the effort. You will probably come up with an impressively high figure that will give you a definite incentive to learn ways to cut that needless paper out of your life and the lives of others you deal with.

DO NOT CUT TOO MUCH

You may be tempted to cut out paperwork "cold turkey" once you learn just how much its compilation, dissemination, and use is costing you and your firm. But such a paperwork backlash is overkill. Certain things must be communicated in person, but this process takes time too, and it does not provide the permanent record that correspondence does.

As a rule of thumb, here is how you can cut your paperwork selectively: If the item can be handled in twenty "people-minutes" or less, do so in person or by phone and forget about writing a report or letter. If it requires more than twenty people-minutes, put it down on paper and use that as your communication medium.

You can avoid some paperwork by using the phone or talking in person, but after that the burden of improvement will lie with streamlining and efficiency. This chapter will give you a number of practical ideas on cutting the fat from your paperwork, your letters, and your reports.

PUT YOUR PAPERWORK ON A DIET

Paperwork is a secure and safe occupation for many—it keeps them from taking risks—and a desk covered with papers looks productive, at least to some people. Lee Grossman, author of *Fat Paper,* suggests that people "overpaper" for the same reasons they overeat—insecurity, fear, and the feeling that something is lacking. Grossman offers a number of solutions to cut down on paperwork. Here are some of the best ones:

Encourage employees to take risks. It is better to act and make a mistake than to hide behind paper and make no decisions. Make sure your people understand that you expect them to learn by doing.

Trust people to report exceptions. You will not have to wade through stacks of routine paper to find real problems if you make it clear to your employees that you want them to report problems and exceptions and not blow-by-blow descriptions of projects that are proceeding without a hitch.

Encourage face-to-face contact. Do not write a memo when you can make your point in person. Make your word your bond, and expect this from others. Do not feel that you always have to "cover your anatomy" with multiple memos.

Explain what should be kept. Many secretaries have been taught to keep everything unless told otherwise. You will have an entire bank of file cabinets unless you toss away more than you save.

Give incentives for cutting paperwork. Encourage employees to search out worthless forms and reports and suggest how they could be eliminated. Offer financial rewards for success in this area.

Control the photocopier. Resist the temptation to have the fastest, clearest photocopier available. You will find that the better the machine, the more photocopies people make. Remember that the paperwork explosion began with the invention of the dry, plain-paper copier. Do not let it rule your office.

ZERO-BASED PAPERWORK PLANNING

The popular zero-based management theories can be applied to bureaucratic paperwork. Say you had to eliminate all the forms you habitually fill out to get work done by other departments and to report to others on your department's activities. Which ones would you want to, and need to, reinstitute? Can you consolidate information that different departments need on one all-inclusive report? Which forms seem to do nothing but take up time? Are you sure anyone still reads or uses them? Share your findings with others. You may find that a number of those "must-do" forms are long since outdated and useless to all.

WRITE CLEARLY AND CUT YOUR WRITING TIME

Here are some tips on getting your writing done in less time and making sure you get your points across in such a way that people read your reports and letters—and act upon them.

Avoid Writer's Block

A sales manager in an electronics manufacturing company gives this advice for those who cannot get started with their writing:

> Writing was a chore for me until I found an easy six-step approach: (1) *think* about what you want the finished piece to look like; (2) *prime yourself* with the facts, ideas, and benefits you want to use; (3) *write* a paragraph or a page on each major point [and] keep them all on separate sheets of paper; (4) *shuffle* them around until the arrangement makes sense; (5) *write* any introductions or bridge-building material you need to link the major pieces together; (6) *proofread* aloud. Now my writing is a pleasure, and it seems to be very much more effective than before.

Make Sure People Read What You Write

Studies show that the most appealing items in a stack are read first. Short, snappy reading material is most appealing to most people. So set up your reports and letters with lots of spaces, bold type, short paragraphs, and short sentences. And if you must write a long report, attach a cover page with a short summary or introduction.

When sending a letter, take a tip from the direct-mail industry to gain quick readership. Have your letters folded with the head out so no one wastes time unfolding your letter to get your ideas.

Do Not Write It Twice

Here are some ways to avoid composing the same letters or reports more than once.

(1) Retain copies of your best memos, letters, and reports. Modify them instead of starting from scratch when a new writing occasion comes up.

(2) Keep this file of starter memos, letters, and the like in two identical loose-leaf notebooks—one for your reference and one for your typist's. The notebooks should be organized by topic and numbered so that individual paragraphs can be identified as well as entire letters and reports.

(3) Refer to the paragraph or letter number you want to use, and dictate any additional comments you need to make. Let your typist take it from there, creating a new letter from your verbal cut-and-paste job.

(4) If you have some literature to distribute, or cost information or other facts that you send out repeatedly, make sure that as much as possible is preprinted so that you can avoid repetitive typing.

Write One-Sentence Letters

Some time-management experts say that no letter needs to be longer than one sentence—or at most, one paragraph. You may not be able to reach this goal, but striving toward it will help you cut the excess verbiage from your correspondence.

The one-sentence summary can apply to reports as well. How about a one-sentence memo to explain the outcome of a project? And adding a one-sentence summary to the beginning of each report will serve two purposes: you will know that everyone has an overview of your material, and if the summary is intriguing, it may spark increased readership of the entire report.

TIPS FOR A BUSINESSLIKE
COMMUNICATION IMAGE

Transmit your dedication to effective time management through your business stationery and style. For instance, print on your business cards and stationery the hours you accept and return phone calls. List the hours during which you will accept appointments.

Make sure your letterhead and card are complete with your full address, zip code, area code, and phone number. If your location is not well known, add a small vicinity map or directions on your letterhead or the back of your card.

If you move, send your change of address on ready-made Rolodex cards. Do the same when sending an introductory note to a prospective client.

When handwriting a reply on the original you received (thus saving typing a formal letter), stamp on the original "We have kept a copy" so that your correspondent knows you are not dismissing the idea. (Of course, make sure that such a copy is kept.)

WAYS TO CUT THE COST
OF BUSINESS LETTERS

Use telegrams or mailgrams instead of business letters when you want to make an impression. You may even save money, because the telegram format forces you to be terse, and your secretary will not have to type a letter-perfect copy.

Another letter-saver is the postcard. Get yourself a batch of standard postcard formats with fill-in blanks for things such as sending for literature, acknowledgment of correspondence that you cannot yet fully respond to, confirmation of appointments, and enclosure with something you want to pass on to someone else.

Letters Checklist

Make a checklist for letters that you write often—for instance, instructions to a supplier. That way, you will not find yourself writing additional letters to add forgotten points or clarify vaguely stated expectations.

Memo Format Letters

Your letters will be easy to file if you add a line after the address that states what the subject is. It will help put your reader in the right frame of mind. You might also highlight important points with a yellow marker to help your reader see what you want most to get across.

Perhaps you will want to go a step further to an actual memo format for your letters, using "To," "From," and "Subject" headings in caps instead of a salutation. To get the most out of this style, make sure your memo-letters are no more than a page in length. If they must be longer than this, a one-paragraph summary labeled as such will be helpful to you and the recipient. Put it at the beginning of the letter.

Another way to save time and effort with this style is to end the letter with your handwritten initials only, saving retyping of your name, title, and all that extra information. When your letters are folded (head out, as suggested earlier), make sure that they are placed into the envelope facing the rear so that when they are opened, they do not have to be turned around.

Canned Letters

If you do not feel confident creating your own book of standard letters, you might want to try a book by L. W. Frailey, *Handbook of Business Letters*. It contains 761 indexed letters for every purpose from appreciation to credit and collections.

Neat Penmanship

A branch manager of a commercial bank wrote *Execu-Time* with this comment: "Poor penmanship is a terrible time-waster. Bank people used to spend hours puzzling out my chicken scratches, mistaking words, calling to check, and so forth. Now I take a few extra seconds to write clearly, because I know it will save minutes, even hours, down the line."

KNOW YOUR PAPERWORK "PRIME TIME"

A number of people have written *Execu-Time* to tell us they have found the perfect time of day for writing and other paperwork. But the times they favor are all different, leading us to believe that there is a paperwork prime time but that it varies from person to person. We have gathered that there are three best times, depending on your preference:

Early morning. Some people find that since paperwork takes a good part of their time, they like to tackle it early and get it out of the way. This means that many of their more important writing jobs can be completed on the same day they are started.

Noon. Other people find that crisis time comes in the morning and afternoon, but at lunchtime the interruptions cease for a bit while people eat. They take a quiet hour at lunchtime and do their paperwork during the lull.

Late afternoon. Another group contends that most paperwork is routine and easy, not to mention repetitive and tedious. They prefer to save it for the hours when they are winding down, after their peak energy has been exhausted for the day.

HOW-TO'S FOR PAPERWORK

Here are some more down-to-earth ideas to help you cope with that mountain of paper in your office:

Do not use paper to discuss or argue. It is a time-waster. Use memos and letters to confirm discussions you have had in person or on the phone.

Standardize formats for memos and letters. That way, you will always know where to look for the source of the correspondence, the subject, date, and so on. Make sure all secretaries and typists know what the standard form is and that they use it.

Do not use unnecessary memos. The training director of a large manufacturing company did an interesting piece of research: "Most of our executives come to me with the problem of too much routine office paperwork. No amount of training could eliminate the paper. Finally, I investigated and found 37 percent of the copies we passed around were 'For Your Information Only'—in other words, unnecessary. We took steps to cut them out and reduced executive paperwork time by 25 percent!"

Cut memo volume two ways. Either send one copy and have it routed to three or four concerned people or put it on the bulletin board and make sure that your people know they must check there periodically for news.

Sort paperwork. An *Execu-Time* reader from Massachusetts offered this hint: "I have my secretary divide mail into four categories: (1) Immediate Action; (2) Pending Action (needs research); (3) File or Distribute; (4) Trash. I find these will cover everything and save everyone time."

If the system above does not appeal to you, try this one, devised by an engineering director:

> I handle the flow of paperwork with a sorting system I developed over the years. As paper comes in, I pile it *in decreasing order of importance*: (1) Work I can and should do myself right now. I handle that as I see it. (2) Work I can and should handle myself, but takes more than a few minutes. These I get started, then file for follow-up. (3) Tasks I can delegate. These I accumulate for a day or two, then delegate in bunches at my staff meetings. (4) Tasks I want to do, but can reasonably delay. These I file in a tickler for future action. (5) Paper to file for reference. My secretary takes this pile away. (6) Material to read once and throw away. I save that for travel time and free minutes that show up throughout the day. Finally, the biggest pile is stuff I can throw away without even reading it. I chuck this out immediately, and it never gets a chance to clog my paperwork system.

Do not even read your letters. A president of a large conglomerate says, "I learned years ago not to write my own letters. But just last month I learned not even to read or sign them. I make a note on what I want to say, and my trained assistant sends it out just the way I would have."

Use postcards. Here is a tip from a management consultant: "I used to load down my pockets and briefcase with scrawled notes on little bits of paper, reminders to talk with various people about specific things. Maybe I'd copy them over into my daybook later, or maybe I'd lose them. Either way was ineffective. Now I carry blank postcards all the time. Whenever I think of an item, I jot a note on a postcard, address it to the appropriate person, and mail them all once a day. They're immediately, and most effortlessly, off my mind. And next thing I know, someone's on the phone or writing with the information I wanted."

Make it easy for your correspondent to respond. A military

officer came up with this suggestion: "I save time and clarify communications in my letters and memos by clearly stating my questions and leaving check-off boxes for possible answers. For example: 'Are lost time days counted ( ) per assembly or ( ) per calendar day?' Formulating simple questions and answers clarifies my thinking and helps the recipient understand and answer informally. My format seems to encourage people to respond immediately rather than to put off answering."

To save paperwork, use a "speed memo" sticker or rubber stamp. The idea is to speed handling of paperwork by writing your reply right on the original. Simply copy the original and your reply on a photocopy for your file and return the original to your correspondent. The sticker goes on the letter or memo to explain what you are doing, so the recipient does not feel slighted. The sticker or stamp might read "SPEED REPLY— In order to give you the fastest possible response, we have made these marginal notes. In this instance we believe you prefer speed to formality." Ask your local office-supply firm to make something similar.

Turn any piece of paper into a speed memo with this sticker at the top. Or add it to your standard memo format to make it more noticeable and to receive faster action. Your correspondent may well pick up on this and respond faster to your inquiry.

Use window envelopes. The risk manager of a large insurance organization came up with this idea: "I've saved hundreds of hours over the years simply by extensive use of window envelopes. By refolding letters so that the address shows through the window, you eliminate scads of unnecessary typing. I make a self-addressed envelope by taping my business card behind the window. And don't forget, windows reduce the chance of typing error by 50 percent or more."

Touch each item once only. Put a dot in the corner of each piece of paper as it crosses your desk. Perhaps you could use red for high-priority items and blue for less important things.

Try to avoid touching any item more than once. In other words, decide what is to be done with it the first time you look at it. File it, delegate it, or dispose of it yourself, one way or another. To test yourself on this, mark another dot each time you pick up the item and put it back down without dealing with it.

Be smart about what you take home. It is a good idea to read complex idea reports in the quiet of your own home. You can also do some of your more complicated writing at home if it is peaceful. And some people do find the best of the trade publications fun to read. But do not overload your briefcase; it can be discouraging and depressing.

Get prepared on the way from the airport. If you travel frequently and have a company driver to pick you up, have the driver bring you a packet of materials prepared by your secretary to sum up the action in your absence. Read it on the drive back and get ready to step into the swing of things immediately.

Keep the in-basket circulating. Make sure you have an empty in-basket several times a day and always last thing at night. Do not become so involved in your To Do list that you ignore fast-breaking developments you may find in your maturing in-basket. This does not mean you have to stop work: ask your assistant to see to this task and present you with the important news.

Here are some of the best hints we have learned from Jim Atkins, time manager and editor of the *Telephone Marketing Report*:

Cover only one topic per memo, in most cases. If you must include more, list topics by number.

Label all paperwork with a *T* (for "*They* want something") or an *I* (for "*I* want something"). If "they" want something, let them do the work, supply the information, make the offer, and so on. You follow up on *I* paperwork until you get what you want.

Get an unlisted direct telephone line, and give people this number to speed communications. For example, one top executive wrote in reply to a letter: "Here's my unlisted personal phone. Call until you get me." The phone line slashed through paperwork and saved days.

Use creative procrastination. Example 1: A staff member has a good idea, but you cannot use it now because advertising money is already committed for the next six months. Tell your colleague to hold the idea for five months and then resubmit. This way, he or she keeps the paperwork and may do more work on the idea. You get it at just the right time.

Example 2: You owe a lengthy report to some prospect. Rather than do the paperwork and prepare the report in total, you put together a one-sheet summary of the different options, packages, and cost approximations. Once they clarify their thinking, you prepare a full-scale report geared to their interests and assumptions.

Let someone else do your writing and research for projects such as articles, speeches, reports, and whatever takes a lot of your time. If you do not have a staff person who can handle this for you, call your local newspaper and speak to the business editor. Ask if they can do the job or if they can recommend someone to do it. You can also contact the president of the National Press Club, in Washington, D.C., who will, without charge, list the work you need done in the Press Club newsletter, which goes to thousands of the nation's top reporters and writers. You may also be able to find a writing service in a city near you that can handle the work at less cost than your own time is worth.

Save others' time and help them to save yours. Send out a carbon or photocopy with your original letter and mark it with a rubber stamp that says, "To save time an extra copy of this letter is enclosed. Please use the back for your reply and save us both from extra paperwork."

Avoid going to the filing cabinet more than once per

project. Clip the entire file to the current item, and let it travel around the office until the project is completed. If necessary, you can duplicate key items initially just in case of loss.

Use colors to signal different kinds of paperwork: accounting, sales, shipping, routine memos, and special announcements. The colors let you sort through paperwork faster, speed routing, and facilitate handling all along the line.

10.

FILING

Lt may be that you have rigged up your own filing system through trial and error, or perhaps you rely on secretaries to file according to the method they learned in school. But if you are losing things or taking too long to find them or if your files are bulging with items you never refer to, this chapter is a "must" for you.

A good filing system is vital to the time manager for three main reasons:

You lose time and money when things are hard to locate. The cost of filing supplies and equipment is very low compared with the personnel time lost when an important item is impossible to find in the files.

You become confused when file folders are labeled improp-

erly. Some people file too much under one general topic, while others file "distant relatives" together, using some logic that is soon lost to them.

You can avoid a bit of stress, because you do not have to keep everything in your head. Files can be more than just inactive repositories of paper. You can set up To Do files, "tickler" files, "follow-up" files, and more.

EXECUTIVE INFORMATION SYSTEM

Every facet of an executive's job begins with paperwork. Amazing as it seems, the filing systems in the United States gain paper at the rate of 1 million new pages per minute. If you do not have a well-planned filing system of your own, it may seem to you as if about half of them cross your desk.

Execu-Time research shows that a large percentage of executives deal with filing on a haphazard basis. Even executives with some sort of filing system in place feel they could improve their accuracy and retrieval time. This six-section filing system was designed to help you avoid forgetting things, to reduce clutter and distractions, and to make sure you can retrieve things quickly. This system has been proven to be simple and automatic. It requires a minimum of effort, thought, and action.

Time File

The time file is for short and easy notes, memos, and items for future study. It is organized by date. Another name for the time file is the "tickler" file, because it tickles your memory when the proper date for action arrives. Just check your tickler file at the beginning of each week and schedule your tickler items into the To Do sheet for each day.

The sample on the next page gives you an idea of what you

TIME (or Tickler) FILE: photocopy this page onto a sheet of 1" x 2¾"/33 to a page address labels (such as made by Xerox or Avery). Then affix the labels to file folders.

January	**February**	**March**
April	**May**	**June**
July	**August**	**September**
October	**November**	**December**
1 2	3 4	5 6
7 8	9 10	11 12
13 14	15 16	17 18
19 20	21 22	23 24
25 26	27 28	29 30 31

Copyright © 1981 Januz Marketing Communications, Inc.

need as file tabs for a time file. (If you would like a set of actual-size file tab labels to use for this purpose, write *Execu-Time* at the address on page 60 for price information.) Make up a folder for each date and a master folder for each month. When you go through your in-basket each day, load up your time file with everything you cannot handle immediately— notes, letters, memos, reports. You should assign dates to items without preassigned deadlines.

The time file frees you from carrying too many items by memory. Each time a future project or a simple phone call comes up that you know you should do something about soon, jot yourself a note and file the note in the proper day's folder. For example:

- Write down reminders of what you must do in the week ahead—schedule meetings, check on plane tickets, and so on.
- Slot in follow-ups on request letters you have sent and projects you have assigned with deadlines, up to a month or so ahead.
- Jog your memory before your important deadlines with a reminder note that appears in the file two to five days before that deadline date. This note can be a safety net if you time its appearance so that you could still finish the project if it has somehow slipped your mind up to that point.
- Use the time file for appointment reminders; stick them in a day in advance so that you can have your meeting materials ready or confirm attendance.

Project File

The project file will help you avoid a desk piled high with current data. Everything related to a certain project should be grouped with it and kept neatly off to one side, or even out of sight, when you are not working on that particular project. Most of the day-to-day materials you work with can be kept in project files. Make sure the name you assign the project explains it completely to you, even if your private project name is different from the corporate one.

Unless the project is one-dimensional and quick to complete, it is an excellent idea to have "sub-files" within each project folder. Some projects may have only four or five sub-files; for instance, if you deal with the Smith family, you might have a John Smith file, a Mary Smith file, and so on. A similar file for the Williams Corporation might, however, have a score of subfiles for items such as life insurance, corporate accounting, marketing, and advertising—whatever separate parts your dealings with Williams comprise. If an item has importance for two or more of these sub-files, simply cross-reference them. This will be explained in more detail later.

Project folders should have a special place in your file drawer or perhaps be kept in a special open file near your desk for easier access. They should be filed in strict alphabetical order. Do not neglect to open project folders when they are needed. This should be the first order of business. Otherwise, you will find stray papers and dog-eared stacks building up before you know it.

If an item is too simple and short to be termed a project, file it in one of three ongoing "priority" folders—priority 1, 2, and 3. Do not let these folders become repositories of busywork or "step-child" jobs. Think of them in this way: *priority 1* means "absolutely vital, to do immediately"; *priority 2*, "work on as soon as possible"; and *priority 3*, "important but not urgent, schedule now for a date in the near future." Put priority folders in your project file so that they will be easily accessible. Schedule them in the time file for transfer to your To Do list when appropriate.

Your "To Finish Today" label goes on a folder that will hold all the items you must finish right away. Having such a folder is much neater than littering your desk with little notes, as well as being much less distracting to you as you work on other projects. As you finish larger tasks and find you have a few minutes left before the next entry time on your To Do list, you can open the folder and do one or two of your Today jobs.

Reading and Research File

A reading and research file acts as an encyclopedia for your field or specialty, holding all the background data that are important to you. Because this file could well be a lifelong project, your file log will be of special importance. (You learn how to set up such a log later in this chapter.)

The reading-research file is organized by subject, with titles of special use to you—"Time Management," "General Business," "Equipment and Services," "Marketing Research," and so on. Make subjects broad or narrow—whatever suits you best. Remember that a file that is overly thick can defeat your purpose unless it is logged systematically and carefully. If you see a file becoming bogged down, do not be afraid to add, subtract, or shuffle.

Keep your file up to date by entering new items every day. If you do not, you will be tempted to let a hopeless backlog build up. You can let it slide to once a week if you are especially faithful about it, or if you add only a few new items a week.

A good bit of the material in the reading-research file will be current reading for you. There are two good ways to keep up with your reading on a timely basis by using the file: (1) *By subject*. At intervals, pull your file on any given subject, and read at a single sitting everything you have filed there recently. (2) *By allotment*. Schedule yourself for a "reading period" daily or weekly, and skim all the new material you have received.

Divide your reading into folders numbered 1, 2, and 3 in order of priority, and one labeled "For Own Reading" for items of interest to you personally. Keep your reading folders easily accessible so that you can skim a few items whenever you have a spare moment. Once you have read them, mark them for filing or tossing. You should be tossing a lot more than you are filing. To make sure your reading folders stay at a manageable size, weed them out once a week. The low-priority folder should be dumped completely of everything you have not had time to read in a week. At this point, finish skimming any high-priority items that are left, and skim or toss secondary items quickly. Then begin refilling the folders for the current week's reading. The "For Own Reading" file is really a home file; transfer what you find at the office to this file for evening reading, for use while on trips, or during spare personal time.

Ideas and Plans File

Having an ideas and plans file will help you avoid forgetting good ideas. It could be called a "Futures" file, because it lists your specific plans for the future as well as your dream projects and accomplishments.

The sample on the next page shows tabs or files labeled "Ideas," "Refined Ideas," "Rough Projects," and "Plans." The general "Ideas" file is the place for your brainstorms—the concepts that wake you up at night and things that come to you from out of the blue. Even if the details seem formidable, write that idea down. You will be happy you did some day when the right combination of circumstances makes it pay off.

Schedule time to review these files periodically so that some of the "Ideas" can be worked into "Refined Ideas," the "Refined Ideas" can become "Rough Projects," and so forth. Once a rough project starts having definite specifications, it should be scheduled according to your project procedure and moved to a project file. The "Plans" part of this file is to be used for

OTHER FILE LABELS: photocopy this page onto a sheet of 1″ x 2¾″/33 to a page address labels (such as made by Xerox or Avery). Then affix the labels to file folders as described. Add additional subject headings as needed in the blank boxes.

Priority One	Priority Two	Priority Three
To Finish Today	For Own Reading	Take With
Reading 1	Reading 2	Reading 3
Reading/Research Log	Ideas	Refined Ideas
Rough Projects	Plans	Trip Folder: _____
Trip Folder: _____	Correspondence 1	Correspondence 2

Copyright © 1981 Januz Marketing Communications, Inc.

objectives, step-by-step systems to reach goals, and other future functions. This file should be updated on a regular basis, and portions of it should be deactivated as they are completed.

Trip File

Trip files provide a home for the information you need about destinations that you visit frequently on business, that you may visit soon, or that you would like to explore as a possible site of business activity. File items in the trip file by geographic location, in alphabetical order by place name. That way, even when you have to leave in a hurry you can pull out the folder marked "Dallas" or "New York" and get all your accumulated data quickly.

Items that might be found in an individual city's trip folder would include previous itinerary or planned one for an upcoming trip, phone numbers, plane tickets, hotel confirmations, contracts, and working papers. As you can see, the general trip file becomes a specific trip aid when you outfit it with the items you need when you are traveling.

If you get in the habit of taking a trip file with you—even for one-night trips to the next town—you will find it comforting to know you have a place for reservation confirmations, tickets, and city guides, and you will find you arrive prepared, not with a lot of loose ends that could spoil the enjoyment of a smoothly planned trip.

General A–Z File

An *A–Z* file is for storing items that do not concern a specific project but are handy to keep around—maps of the state, charts referring to the organization of your firm or other firms, general financial data, and so on. The folders in this file will have very general titles so that you can locate things without thinking too hard—"Maps," "General Background, Smith Corp.," and the like.

HOW THE FILE LOG WORKS

Notice the accompanying file log form, which can serve as an excellent control on your file structure and use. Fill out the form each time you turn to your files or ask your secretary to get something from them. After about a week of logging, you will have a good list of topics for your file log categories. Do not worry about making a complex entry that spells out everything; just use initials, abbreviations, or code words— whatever you and your secretary can decipher. Using this system, you can find out which files you need most frequently and which categories are easiest to work with. Then when you get a new piece of information to file, you can categorize it according to the list of groupings you have developed for easy retrieval later on.

FILE LOG: complete drawing the bottom of this form and print or photocopy it for use as described under "How to Keep a File Log".

File Log

Information Required	Reason

Copyright © 1981 Januz Marketing Communications, Inc.

Here is how to enter reading-research materials in your log: (1) Number each item consecutively, and staple all sheets from one article or report together. (2) Note on your log the item's title, its consecutive number within its file, and the subject categories it relates to. (3) File each item in numerical order in a safe place where it will not deteriorate (magazine storage cartons are good). The items that are of interest but not worth saving can be placed in your reading folder with the word *Toss* on top instead of a log number.

ACTIVE AND INACTIVE FILES

It is important to categorize your files so that you can get to frequently used items quickly, without sifting through items that you hardly ever call for. If you can categorize items on a sliding scale of frequency of use, you will save yourself or your secretary lots of time and aggravation locating things.

Superactive files. Some items you turn to every day or several times a day, such as time files and project files. They should be within your own reach; it is silly to have your secretary running for them constantly. You should set them up in your desk drawer or credenza within arm's length.

Active files. Files that you use several times per week or maybe even once a week are considered active. This category includes your reading file, *A–Z* file, and file for projects recently completed or just gearing up. Make sure you can get to them without going more than a few steps.

Semiactive files. These files are ones you turn to on an irregular basis, but that you do look for every few weeks or so to clear up questions. Examples would be the long-term reading-research files and trip files (unless you travel every week). Put these where you can have access without making a special request, but out of your work area.

Inactive files. These are the files you want to keep, or must keep, for years. Examples would be legal or tax papers and old

Reading/Research Log

Item Name, Source or Author	Item #	Subject	Subject	Subject	Subject	Subject	Subject	Subject	Subject

Copyright © 1981 Januz Marketing Communications, Inc.

project files from years back. These should be carefully la-beled, weeded out, and filed away from your work area. If you have no room in your own office or just outside your office, file them in a storage room. Just make sure you know what is where so that you can call for needed papers without delay. Your file log is essential for this purpose.

HOW TO FILE

Here is a short alphabetical guide to filing any item you come across:

Appointments. Mark the appointed date on your calendar, and file related papers and a reminder in your time file. If the appointment has to do with a project or other file category you have, file related paperwork in its proper place and retrieve it before the appointment; if it is not related to a project, file papers in the time file.

Articles. Number articles consecutively, and mark appropri-ately in the reading-research log. Also cross-reference with re-lated project folders and other areas where the article might shed light. Scan the article during your reading time, but do not digest it unless the information becomes vitally important.

Books. Same procedure as articles. Books should be shelved in your office in numerical order according to your file log, instead of filing them.

Letters. General correspondence goes into the *A–Z* file. If the item relates to a project it goes in the proper project folder. If you need to respond to the letter in the future, put it in your time file. If it contains important research back-ground, file it in the reading-research file or in the *A–Z* file by subject.

Memos. Put memos in the time file according to the date when you must act. Once action is taken, discard or file in the project, trip, or *A–Z* file.

Notes. Same procedure as memos.

Projects. Mark a new folder and start filing as soon as a project begins to shape up. Start with one general folder, and divide papers when the details start becoming important. Keep all folders for the project together—perhaps in a master folder with accordion sides.

Publications. Check the table of contents and the short-item sections for items of special interest. Skim the appealing articles, clip those that seem relevant or valuable, and log them. File in the reading-research file and then discard what is left. Discontinue subscriptions to the publications from which you do not clip much.

Reminders. These notes go in the time file under the appropriate date. Note the item on your calendar, too, if appropriate.

Reports. Regular reports can go into reading file 1. If you do not read them within three weeks, simply file into subject or project folders or discard. If the report is a special one, scan it and then file it for reading. If it relates to a certain project, put it in the project folder with a cross-reference in reading-research so that you will pull it out when reading time comes.

Time Files

- File under the date due or one day before.
- File by the month—everything due in the next thirty days goes in the time file.
- Empty the monthly folder on the first of each month; distribute what is left into proper folders for the following month, project files, and so on.
- Items that will occur more than thirty days hence go into a monthly folder to be broken down in the appropriate month.
- At the end of the day or, at the latest, first thing the next morning, check through the day's folder and

schedule things on your To Do plan. Stick to this plan for an effective day's work.

Trip Files

- Clip items as you see them about destinations for planned or possible business or personal trips.
- File by destination. You may also have folders by airlines, train lines, and ship lines if appropriate.
- Weed out your trip file yearly to eliminate outdated material, uninteresting information, destinations no longer of interest, and so on.

Reading-Research Files

- Number all items consecutively.
- Log items each day or each week. Log them by article title, source and author, item number assigned by you, and subject.
- Weed out your entire reading-research file once a year to eliminate outdated or irrelevant material.

A–Z Files

- If items are important or relevant but have no place in your trip, reading, project, idea, or time files, put them here.
- File by what the item is about, not by what it is.
- Cross-reference items that have several logical applications. For example, an item on your firm's new labor contract might be referenced for "Negotiations," "Unions," or "Personnel." Put the actual item under its most logical heading, and place a note in the other relevant files.

HOW TO CROSS-REFERENCE

Cross-referencing is an important tool for finding an item when you need it. It can act as your "checks and balances" system to help you avoid misfiling or losing documents you need. Here are some pointers:

- Cross-reference whenever an item should be in more than one place in your information system. It should be directly relevant to two or more folders to be cross-referenced. Do not just reference things haphazardly.
- Underline in red, or jot down a note of, the key words that identify where you will file the item and cross-reference it.
- Rather than cross-referencing, if the item is just one or two pages, photocopy it, and place it in each relevant file.
- Multipart forms make a good cross-referencing tool. You only have to fill out the cross-reference location information once and then drop a form copy into each relevant file.
- Granted, cross-referencing will add perhaps 10 percent to the amount of papers you file. But studies show that a well-cross-referenced file can cut the executive's retrieval time by as much as 50 percent.

PURGING

You should plan to throw out paperwork as soon as it is practical to do so. Work out a set of rules on how often you will purge files and how long you will keep reports and other regular materials. Keep a list such as that on page 161 with your file log so that you will remember your rules and act on them:

Purge Instructions

	How often	*Discard all older than*
Time File	_____	_____
Project File	_____	_____
Reading File	_____	_____
Ideas and Plans	_____	_____
Trip Files	_____	_____
A–Z Storage	_____	_____

TIPS ON FILING

Here are some tested ideas from executives with much filing experience as well as experience with the filing methods explained in this chapter.

Clean Out Files

A publisher wanted to test a new time recall system submitted by a manufacturer. He had to remove all of the file folders from the right-hand drawer of his desk to accommodate the new system. The drawer was 23 inches deep, and when the nonpertinent information had been removed to other areas (wastebasket, idea file, low-priority files, and so on) only eight folders remained in the high-priority personal file.

Ask yourself when you last cleaned the file drawers in your desk or credenza. If they are not full of material that you constantly and continuously use, you are wasting time having to weed through the nonessentials. The "Fishing Trip" and

"Vacation" idea folders this publisher found in his desk file drawer hardly rated the priority they were assigned. Some of the folders had not been opened in two or three years.

John Lee's Four D's

Time-management expert John Lee suggests that you evaluate everything that crosses your desk as one of the four *D*'s, for filing purposes: *Drop*—drop the garbage right into the circular file. *Delay*—hold off until later (most of these become drops when you review them). *Delegate*—get somebody else on it and get it off your desk. *Do*—much more manageable when you get the other three *D*'s off your desk. These items can go into the time, reading, or other files for action now or at a scheduled time in the future.

Alphabetical File Alternatives

Unless your business has only one type of item to file—insurance policies, credit applications, whatever—your *A–Z* file may yield up too much general material, even with a good file log. Louis B. Lundborg, a time-management expert of many years' standing in the industry, suggests a filing system based on the way your firm operates with alphabetical sections within each subject category. Each subject category should have its own "life" schedule—that is, its own area on the purge schedule discussed earlier. Categories to consider for your filing subjects could include activities supervised, reports received, reports generated, correspondence, support materials, and interdepartmental activities.

Separate Files

A file of suppliers and a file of civic and board activities are useful categories, depending on your business.

SUPPLIERS FILE

An *Execu-Time* reader wrote:

We have many salesmen who call on us regularly. We began a suppliers' filing system several years ago. In these files we keep pertinent information such as price lists, names and addresses of salesmen, district managers, technical people, and a running diary of each visit or phone call from the salesman, including the important points of discussion. Whenever the salesperson comes in for an appointment, my secretary brings me the pertinent file, and I can quickly review it while the secretary brings the salesperson to my office.

CIVIC-BOARD FILE

The associate publisher of a newspaper said:

I handle information on my civic and board activities by maintaining a three-ring notebook for each organization. Each notebook has a separate section for general board meetings and the activities of each committee. In those sections I retain my own notes, official minutes, and other material that I deem worthy of keeping. The notebooks are color-coded so I can grab the right one fast on the way to a meeting.

11.

DICTATION

The most valuable skill that you can learn to help improve your time management is dictation, and the most valuable tool you can acquire is a portable dictation unit. Those of you who already make it a habit to use a portable recorder probably would not know how to get along without it. But studies show that as many as four out of ten executives write out their letters and memos by hand before turning them over for typing.

If you are one of these handwriters, try a little test to show yourself how much time you are wasting. How many words per minute can you write (or type if that is what you have been doing)—twenty? thirty? Perhaps sixty if you are a pretty fair typist? That is not too fast when you consider that the spoken word comes out at about 150 words per minute.

If you dictate directly to your secretary, there is room for improvement, since you are probably capable of speaking twice as fast as he or she is able to take down your words. If you are handwriting, you can quadruple your dictation speed by switching to dictation equipment; if you are dictating directly, you can double your speed by using such equipment.

The convenience factor is important, too. The newer dictation machines are smaller than a pack of cigarettes and can be used anywhere, at all times for note-taking, delegating, or dictating.

If your assistant or secretary rebels at the thought of using dictating equipment, propose a test for several weeks. Some firms will give you a test unit, or "loaner," to try for a while before you purchase. Many stenographers find using the dictating machine a freeing experience for them, too, since they can transcribe and type to suit their own daily schedules.

DICTATION-MACHINE USES

With tapes that pop in and out, you can keep using different tapes for different subjects—one for expenses, another for ideas, a third for correspondence and notes to people you delegate to. With the tiny idea-capsule type of cassettes, you can carry a number in a very small space. They are so small that you can easily mail them back for transcribing if you are on the road.

Keep a record of meetings on tape. Sometimes you can eliminate the need for minutes if you record the meeting. That way, you will have a true record of what went on, although you need not transcribe it unless a question comes up later. Make it known that you save these tapes for an agreed-upon length of time and then erase them to use again.

Have people report to you on tape. The chief operating

officer of a supermarket chain told *Execu-Time*, "I used to waste time requiring written reports from my subordinates, then reading them during valuable office or home hours. Now I ask them to dictate their reports, and I listen directly to their cassettes while I drive to work. This saves input and output time, and usually results in better understanding, too."

Record instructions for staff on tape. You can transfer work to your staffers easily by recording instructions on a cassette for them. For example, go through your mail and explain on tape what needs to be done with each item. Then give the cassette and the mail to your secretary. If you are working late and want to leave some instructions for staffers, leave the To Do list on a cassette and your secretary or assistant can listen to it first thing in the morning.

Doctors find a special use for dictation. A physician who reads *Execu-Time* explains his dictation time-saver: "I use a portable cassette recorder to dictate my findings and recommendations in the presence of each patient. The dictation saves me time and gives me three other advantages: I get the work done while the facts are fresh in my mind; I let my patient know exactly what I'm saying about him to myself or to others; and in the case of instructions, I double the impact by letting the patients hear me dictate them, and later handing them the typewritten copy."

DICTATE EFFECTIVELY

If you are a novice at dictation, you may need some pointers on how to dictate effectively. There are a number of books devoted wholly to this subject; you can pick one up in your local library or bookstore. But here you will find some basics, which will be enough to head you in the right direction.

Here are some objectives and reminders from Merrill Douglass, a Michigan time-management expert, that will help you keep on track when you dictate.

Preparation requires you to be clear about your objectives and to outline them. Have all necessary references at hand when you begin. Allow enough time to dictate effectively without interruption. Execution should begin with instructions: whether it is a letter or memo, what kind of letterhead, and so on. Speak distinctly. Write for the recipient—be conversational, but concise. Spell difficult words for the transcriber.

MIKE FRIGHT

Some people never get started dictating because they have a phobia about microphones. A gradual approach may work best. Start with simple one-sentence memos and then dictate three- or four-paragraph directives. When a longer report is required, prepare and dictate it in sections that you have outlined in advance. You may fool yourself and become an ardent advocate of the very microphone you tried to stay away from.

SEVEN STEPS TO BETTER DICTATION

Auren Uris is an expert in memo-writing and other management techniques. His seven steps will help even the beginner dictate successfully with a bit of planning:

Decide what to dictate. The longer the job, the greater your potential for time savings. Memos and other jobs with formats are ideal because your secretary can fill in the beginning and the end and you can just dictate the meat.

Steno or machine? Machines are a bit harder to correct than a human being, but you can do it by playing back or just saying, "Scratch that completely." You must be clear with a machine; the transcriber cannot tell you how garbled the sound is until it is too late.

Organization. Collect all your information and reference material, then make a rough outline. Open books to the pages you will refer to and get comfortable. Then you are ready to start.

Getting started. Recheck your preparations to enhance confidence. Plug in with something easy, just to get started talking.

Continuing the effort. Follow your outline exactly; do not let yourself ramble. If you get nervous, try alternate means. (Use a machine if a secretary bothers you, a human being if the machine seems too impersonal.) If you get stuck on a word or idea, just say, "Something, something," and continue; fix it on the typed draft later.

Improving your copy. Normally you should strive to have the first draft be the final one. But for important papers, get a transcript and perfect the draft. Cut repetition and overwriting. Remember your mistakes and try to avoid them when you dictate next time.

Improving your technique. Practice often until your portable cassette recorder is an indispensable aid. Spot your weak points by studying the typed copy. Improve your outlines and concentration to make the end product more effective.

12.

READING AND SPEED READING

This discussion of reading has three main time-management goals: to help you reduce the amount of reading you need to do; to teach you to maximize retention of what you do read; and to assist you in reading faster.

READING

The first piece of advice you need is this: eliminate reading material that confuses the issue and does not gain anything for you. Stop magazine subscriptions to publications that you do not read; talk to the people who send you reports that have no application for you and have your name crossed off their lists; check anything that is stacked up in your reading file over a period of time and do what you can to get rid of it.

Next, learn to be selective about what you read. Start with the summaries of reports or books; do not launch right in until you see if this is truly a work of interest or relevance to you. Check the beginning and the end of each section before reading the middle; introductions and chapter summaries will help you determine if the presentation is good reading for you. Other summary areas of use include the table of contents, section or chapter headings, and lead paragraphs.

Third, you can cut the amount of material you read by delegating some reading to your assistant or even to a paid reader. Have your delegate summarize or outline important facts from relevant works. This will save you time and groom your people for better things as well.

If you cannot arrange for someone to read for you, you might try to bargain with your colleagues for cooperative reading. Each of you could read a trade publication, journal, or general report of interest and then hold a half-hour meeting weekly to impart the highlights of each publication.

Another time-saver ties in with your reading-research folder. When you run across an article or item of interest, simply mark it by topic and file it in your reading-research file. Then, when the time comes to read all items on this topic, you will read the article with related material. You will retain more about the topic by reading widely on it all at once than by getting snatches of information on the topic from time to time.

A computer company manufacturing executive wrote *Execu-Time* with his plan for prescreening reading: "I save time by getting my secretary to prescreen all my reading. I've taught her to give me mail, journals, memos, and anything else on paper in one of four categories: *(a)* requires immediate action or decision; *(b)* useful information for background or future use; *(c)* routine reading, optional; and *(d)* applies to an on-going project, specified. She handles everything else that comes in. I read only what's important and useful—a tremendous time-saver."

A health center officer from Iowa lightens the reading load this way: "Instead of reviewing each magazine that comes into the office, I ask for a list of the magazines that come into the library. From that list I identify those from which I want a copy of the table of contents. The librarian furnishes these copies and I simply check off all of those articles which I wish to have sent over for reading. This saves considerable time in reviewing all the magazines and also assists in circulation of timely publications."

Another way to get a helpful summary of relevant news and opinion is to subscribe to newsletters in your field of interest. *Boardroom Reports* is an excellent general business newsletter, and *Execu-Time* is a twice-monthly summary of time-management concepts and methods. Check around for newsletters in your area of business or expertise.

Here are a few more ideas that you can implement right away to make sure you are getting the most you can out of the least possible reading time:

Read while you walk. A Spokane, Washington, consultant combines his walking break with a reading period for material of immediate interest that comes in each morning. After a morning's concentration, he loads his pockets with reading material and walks out into a local park. On the way he skims the material and then at a park bench reads in-depth the items that deserve attention. That way he gets some exercise and fresh air, gets a new perspective by leaving the office, and completes his daily necessity reading as well.

Read fifteen minutes a day. How long has it been since you read a book on a subject important to your field of business? If it has been a while, you may feel that you do not have the time to devote to books, especially technical ones.

But time-management expert Ron Davis says that just fifteen minutes of reading per day will allow you to read (or at least scan) fifty books per year. In many fields, that means a year's reading will put you on top of everything worthwhile that is available in print. In other, more complex fields, it will put you way ahead of others who do not keep up with the latest developments.

Get a quick overview. Say that you need to write a report about a subject you are not familiar with. Or maybe a new product is in the developmental stage and you want to learn about the raw materials that go into it. If the topic is not one you are used to working with, you could spend endless hours searching out the simple, basic information you need. Instead try the children's or junior's department of your library or bookstore. Children's books are almost as well researched as those for adults—and sometimes better. They cut out the long-winded verbiage that keeps you from getting the point fast.

Retain information through repetition. Here is what one *Execu-Time* reader does to retain important facts from his reading: "While many items of information need only one or two readings, I have found that worthwhile items often require repetition. But this need not be a time-waster. For example, I mark in the margins of *Execu-Time* ideas especially pertinent to me. Months later, I quickly review to check my memory and increase the benefits I get from the material. I also read very important items into my cassette recorder, and listen to the tapes while shaving, dressing, driving, etc. I may spend 10 percent more time on an item this way, but I get 80 percent more benefits than I would from a quick reading and subsequent forgetting."

Request short reports. Keep writing and reading to a minimum by demanding that each item fit on one double-spaced page. You can always look up the detailed background or data should it become necessary.

Make notes on reports. When you read a long report, note main points, ideas, and analysis in the margins. Ask your secretary to type them up and staple the paper to the front of your report before it is filed; this way you will have an instant review to read if you should call for the report again.

SPEED READING

A speed-reading course could help you peel hours off the time you spend keeping up with necessary reading. Check your local college or university for availability of a reasonably priced speed-reading class. Or to get started, read this speed-reading summary. This report covers some basics from experts in speed reading. If you cannot take a speed-reading course locally, these basics may help you get more from your reading in the shortest possible time.

Stop Moving Your Lips When You Read

If you have the bad habit of moving your lips as you read, this is the first thing you need to work on. Speed-reading expert Judith F. Larson suggests that you practice reading simple newspaper articles while saying something else—the numbers 1 through 4, for instance, or the first few words of a familiar poem. At first, you may not be able to comprehend what you are reading without your crutch, but with practice you can eliminate lip movements as you read.

Four Kinds of Reading

You should recognize that different reading materials require different levels of attention and concentration. Walter B. Pitkin breaks the types of reading down into four categories:

Light reading. Examples are newspapers and simple fiction. You should be able to read 5 or 6 words per second.

Average reading. Serious news articles and trade journals. Read 4 words per second.

Solid reading. Technical material not in your own field. Slow down to 3 words per second.

Heavy reading. Technical discussions of new subjects that you must master. Read 6,000 words per hour.

Try to accelerate your reading speed of easy material—save your intense reading skills for those times when you truly need to do deep study.

Preview and Then Read

You can save yourself needless reading time by previewing materials and rejecting those not worth careful perusal. Check the title, read any subheadings, and then check to see who the author is—an expert or someone who is restating the thought of others? Examine illustrations and captions. Read the first few paragraphs to catch the theme and pace of the piece. Then read all topic sentences. This will be enough to satisfy your needs from a good deal of the material you come across. Those few books and articles that deserve closer attention can be read in depth.

13.

TRAVELING

If travel—even daily commuting or trips around town—is a part of your professional life you owe it to yourself to think things through and cover that ground as efficiently as possible. Here are some hints on traveling as effectively as you can—around the city or around the world.

LOCAL TRAVEL

The daily commute does not have to be a grind if you plan for it. Leave a bit earlier than the rush so that you get a seat on the bus or train or miss the heavy traffic on the expressway.

If you drive to work, carry a cassette player so that you can listen to books, lectures from seminars in your field, or "positive mental attitude" talks to prime your mind for a productive day.

Before you leave the house by car, make sure that you have a simple emergency kit with you. Include such items as change, postage stamps, bandages, note paper, a few envelopes, and your address book. You will be prepared for emergencies.

An *Execu-Time* reader gave us this idea for a kit for those who must travel to various meetings on unrelated subjects. Follow this advice and you will avoid a last-minute scramble for the right notebook, background information agendas, and the like. "Keep a separate, inexpensive briefcase or folder for each meeting you must attend. Each one should contain your 'permanent' materials for the organization, such as by-laws, reference materials, etc., plus more current 'subject' files on individual projects."

BUSINESS TRIPS BY CAR

Before you hit the road next time, make sure you have prepared yourself for that business trip in a time-wise way. When traveling by car, a number of easy preparatory steps will save you time, worry, and inconvenience:

Equip your car. A citizens-band radio is a good investment because you can find out about bad road conditions, get alternate routes, and summon help in an emergency.

Other important car equipment should include a comfortable driver's seat (check when you buy the car, or invest in a new back-support bucket seat if your car can accommodate it); toll money and a holder to keep it handy; a highway emergency kit; and—if you do a lot of freeway driving—cruise control.

Know where you are going. Take time to plan your route

before you leave. See if you can make some extra, productive stops without going out of your way. Call a few prospects or clients who are in the area to which you will be going and try to set up appointments that will use your travel time to the fullest advantage.

Get yourself a road atlas and a supply of local maps for the area you cover. Make sure you know all the details of how to get to your client's office; just knowing how to get to Podunk without street directions can save much time. Ask about one-way streets and other traffic patterns, too.

Use your driving time effectively. Take along some cassettes or tune to an all-news radio station. Do not forget your dictaphone for memos or notes.

Give yourself ten extra minutes on your way to important meetings or appointments. If you arrive on time, do a short task you have brought along or read a trade publication. The peace of mind of knowing you are not going to be late will help you enter the meeting in a much better mood.

Trick yourself into leaving on time. As time expert Alan Lakein reminds us, the important factor in getting to an appointment on time is the time that you leave your office to get there. So do not write the appointment time on your calendar or To Do lists. Instead, record the time at which you will need to leave in order to make it comfortably. Make your secretary aware of this, too, or set a timer for yourself. Promptness is one of the best time-management traits you can cultivate, as you will save yourself needless anxiety and arrive calm and ready to work.

Get someone else to drive. Try to get others to drive when several of you are traveling by car on business together. You will arrive fresher, and you will be able to read, dictate into your portable recorder, or even get reports from others in the car and make notes as you ride along. If you carpool, pay somebody else to do the driving for the same reasons.

OUT-OF-TOWN TRAVEL

Don Korn, editor of a business travel newsletter, has these tips to ease your business travel routine:

Pretrip Planning

Have a trip file. For every major business trip and for minor ones that you make on a regular basis, you should catalog hotels, along with rates and impressions you and others have of them; restaurant reviews; business background; information on special events; and so on. A good idea for this file is to subscribe to the local city magazine and read over the latest issue before you leave for the town. When you go out of town, take the appropriate file with you for reference.

Have a travel kit ready to go at all times. If you travel frequently, have ready the toiletries, underwear, nonperishable medication, glasses, flashlight, and business cards you will need. You might even keep a suit and shirt-tie combination at the office if you travel frequently enough to warrant it. Then when it is time to travel, a few quick additions of clothing and files is all you will need.

Cultivate a good travel agent. Or get to know your company's travel manager if you have one. This person will do a much better job of booking your travel than you can do for yourself. You may need to shop around a bit until you find a travel agent who will provide all the nice little extras, but once you do find the right agency, it can save you a great deal of time and uncertainty.

Do not overschedule. In a strange town, everything will run longer than you anticipate, because of travel time between appointments, if nothing else. Leave extra time for preparation and optional activities. Do not rush to fill every minute without allowing yourself breathing space or margin for error.

Leave an itinerary. This saves time for your secretary and your spouse, so make sure they each have a copy. Make sure the listing is complete with phone numbers of hotels, branch offices, and the like. This way, if there is an urgent personal or business message for you, you stand a good chance of getting it before it is too late.

Air Travel

Book yourself on extra flights. If you miss a flight, you are trapped unless you can hop the next one for sure. Airlines overbook, so do not feel guilty about doing the same, especially in peak periods. That way, if you are late, you will have a confirmed seat on a later flight, and if you should be "bumped," you will have an option, too.

Try to reserve your seat when you reserve your flight. American, TWA, and United can give you a boarding pass for a return or connecting flight ahead of time, to save time waiting in lines.

Join an airline club or two. You will be able to use a VIP lounge and have an attendant keep track of your coat and bags and check your flight, while you relax in a comfortable chair and make phone calls, hold meetings, or enjoy a quiet meal. The club will also take your phone messages.

Get the airlines' "preferred" phone numbers. If you are a frequent traveler on an airline or a member of their club, you can get access to direct lines that are open when the public lines are tied up. If all the big-city lines are busy, try calling a nearby smaller town for the same information, and you will get through much faster.

Cut down on layovers and plane changes. A direct flight with a stop is preferable to a plane change. Carry a pocket flight guide to check these things instantly. If the flight you are booked for shows signs of being very late or being canceled, you will be able to check your options yourself.

Do not expect to do heavy business while waiting for a flight. Carry your mail and magazines or trade publications to leaf through at this time. Wait until the last call to board if you have a guaranteed seat marked on your boarding pass; there is no sense standing and waiting when you could be reading or working in your seat at the gate.

Do not quit working when the plane lands. You know from experience that taxiing can take time. Keep reading or working until the plane makes the gate, and then get out. If you are stuck at the back of a long exit line, you will do better to continue working at your seat until the line thins out.

Select an important task to do while airborne. Start as soon as you can after boarding the plane, and get your task out of the way so you can relax or work on lower-priority items.

Consider first class. The fare is 20 percent more, but if you need room to work, and if children and chatty adults distract you, you will find other quiet business travelers in first class, which has better food and service as well. And you can leave the plane first, saving time and aggravation.

Do not check baggage if you can avoid it. Pack carefully and invest in luggage that fits under the seat or in the hanging-bag area. If you must check your luggage, mark it with tape or ribbons so you can spot it fast at the claim area. Use your business address on the tags so that burglars will not have access to your home address and know that your house is empty.

Arrive at the airport at least a half hour before takeoff. This will help you avoid the risk of being bumped or missing the flight. That way, even a traffic jam will not be cause for undue alarm.

Avoid busy times of the day and year. Christmas, Thanksgiving, or winter school vacations are the busiest seasons, and 4:00 P.M. to 7:00 P.M. are the busiest hours at airports, so avoid those times if you can.

Stay away from the larger "hub" airports for connections. Chicago and Atlanta, for example, almost guarantee a delay. Try for nonstop flights or connect at less hectic airports such as Charlotte.

Avoid taking your own car to the airport. If it is necessary, park at a valet lot and have the service drive you to the terminal to avoid the long walk from the parking lot. If you have a company driver, take advantage of this service to get to the airport.

Select an aisle seat as far forward as you can. Unless you need the smoking section, the best seat on wide-bodied planes is the interior aisle far side *(F* in eight-across, G in nine-across).

Take a flight with a full-course meal rather than a snack. That way you will not have to take extra time for a meal.

Renting cars wastes a lot of time. Because of the lines, driving to the rental car lot, and dropping the car off when you are done, you will do better to rely on cabs or limos that you can hop into at will.

Try for airport business meetings when you can. Then you can turn around and fly out to your next destination. If you can, arrange to hold seminars at airport hotels, too. Both of these ideas save you traffic problems.

Don't automatically jump on a plane. Consider the alternatives. In the Northeast, trains may be a better bet for you, because major cities are so close together. Consider the cost in time for the total trip, including going to and from the airport, before you decide a plane is faster.

Car Rental Advice

As we said previously, do not rent a car unless you really have no alternative; it is a time-waster. But if you do need to rent one, make prior arrangements with the rental company and perhaps you can have them pick you up at the airport curb. Ask if the driver can put your luggage in the car and bring it around for you while you sign the papers. Get a good map from the rental counter and consult the counter attendant to find out exactly how to get where you are going. Make sure you are supplied with a full tank of gas when you pick up the car so that you do not have to look around a strange town for a place to get gas and waste time standing in line to buy it. Write down the make and color of the car that you rented so that if your mind goes blank you can find it again. If you get lost, stop immediately and call for more advice. Do not compound your error by driving around looking for a way out.

If you have problems with your rental car, just leave it in a safe spot and go to your next appointment. Inform the rental company when it is convenient for you and have them pick up the car.

Leave sufficient time to turn in your rental car before your flight out. This process can be quite time consuming, and unless you already have your boarding pass, you could easily miss your flight if you try to cut it close.

Hotel Hints

Location is as important in selecting a hotel as it is in buying real estate. If you like a certain hotel or chain, by all means stay there, but make sure you have selected the branch most convenient to the airport or your business. Stay at the same hotels as often as you can so that you will get to know the managers and be eligible for better service, faster check-outs, and other privileges. Ask about express check-out so that you can leave promptly on your last day.

Always guarantee your first night's stay with a credit card when you make your reservation to insure that there will be a room waiting when you arrive. Just remember to call and cancel if your plans change; most hotels require that you do it before 6:00 P.M. on your expected day of arrival if you do not want to be charged. If there is a concierge floor in the hotel, stay there or at least ask about concierge service, which will help you make reservations, get tickets, and find local businesses and contacts without delay. Carry your own alarm clock so that you do not stake the success of your day on a tardy wake-up call.

Before you take the airport limo from your hotel, find out how many stops it will make before it gets to the airport. It may be cheaper than a cab, but much more time-consuming if your hotel is the first of ten stops before the airport.

Entertaining Clients and Dining Out

Do not hesitate to tell a waiter or waitress that you are in a hurry. Ask for your menu with your cocktail order, and order your meal when the cocktail arrives. When dessert and coffee time comes, ask for your check along with that final order.

Note your meal expense on your expense log immediately at the end of the meal—who, where, and why. This is much better than trying to recall it all later.

If in doubt, call for a reservation at a restaurant you are not familiar with. This avoids aggravation if you should happen to drop in on their big "steak fry" night that has been sold out for weeks.

Dine at off-hours for faster service: before noon for lunch; before seven in fine restaurants for dinner.

Do not eat alone when you are on the road. Besides helping avoid loneliness, a business meal will afford a fine opportunity to get to know your associates in a relaxed, unpressured atmosphere. And if you are pressed for time, you can always combine a one-hour lunch with a one-hour meeting and save an hour on your schedule.

INTERNATIONAL TRAVEL IDEAS

International travelers should have their passports and some foreign currency for the destination safely tucked away in their travel kits. And have travel files for your foreign destinations, too. Keep your ears and eyes open for material you can use and contacts in the other country who can help you get your bearings.

When you book that long flight, ask about any time-saving or comfort services you can opt for, such as express check-in, preferred luggage treatment, and quiet zones on the plane.

Some Pacific routes now offer sleeping berths in first class. This is a good investment in rest that will let you arrive at your destination ready for work and not staggering from jet lag.

To get the local currency before you leave home (we recommend fifty dollars' worth), exchange your money at a large bank or the exchange in your own airport. Exchange lines are likely to be long and slow when you get to your destination.

The Concorde is more expensive than first class, but if the time you save—3.5 to 4 hours of flying time—is worth several hundred dollars to you, by all means opt for the Concorde.

Utilize the local American embassy, and contact the telephone company for what help they can give you. The embassy can help you make business connections, and the telephone company can help you find out how to dial direct calls. Be aware, however, that foreign phone service is not as efficient as ours, and you may encounter language problems as well.

14.

DEALING WITH INTERRUPTIONS

There is no such thing as a perfectly calm executive behind a perfectly clear desk—at least not at the middle-management level. So with that myth tucked away for good, let us proceed to find as many ways as possible to deal effectively with those inevitable interruptions, to keep them to a minimum, and to carve out a quiet hour each day for work that must be done in private.

You can waste a lot of valuable time wishing for total control over your day. Albert Shapero, professor of management at the University of Texas in Austin, says that "operations people are constantly handling the unexpected. And that's what they are there for." If you accept this fact, you can try for the optimum in "time stretchers" for yourself—thirty, sixty, or ninety minutes at a time.

Studies show that executives will be interrupted once every eight minutes unless they do something to shield themselves. Do not let others cut you down to an eight-minute attention span. And when those interruptions are inevitable, make sure that you know how to pick up again without delay.

HOW TO PICK UP THE THREADS

When you are interrupted, take a few seconds to write yourself a reminder of what you were doing, thinking, or about to say. Then give full attention to the interruption; you will not have to keep half your mind on the thing you will be returning to. Once the interruption is finished, read your note and get back to work.

Another idea is to understand the pattern of your interruptions so that you can cut down on them. Dr. Robert Riley, consultant and professor of business administration at the University of Cincinnati, says interruptions have three distinct parts, including preliminary socializing, a statement of the reason for the interruption, and final socializing. As you can see, the socializing time on either side of the core could well take more time than the reason itself.

You can cut this time factor by taking three steps: (1) As soon as the person appears, ask pleasantly for the reason for the interruption. Do not allow time to start in on the weather, the ball score, or the office gossip. (2) Having made a note of what you were doing before the interruption, direct all your attention to the reason for the interruption, giving direction, delegating, or solving the problem immediately. (3) Finish up while you still have the floor with a comment such as "I'm glad that's settled. Now I can get back to this report, which is due this afternoon." Word this to fit your work schedule, but make it clear that the work on your desk is top-priority. Then, with a smile to the interrupter, begin working on your project again.

As you can see, it is not necessary to be rude, just firm. A smile can soften your words. Most of those who interrupt you will be relieved to find they can get in and out without "over-kill socializing." After all, they have projects waiting too.

PLAN YOUR INTERRUPTION SCHEDULE

Previous chapters have taught you skills for time-log planning and for appreciating your own highs and lows. Make sure that you save your peak output periods for top-priority projects. That is when your door should be closed, if at all possible, and your calls and visits held for later.

Most of us also have a time of day when we feel more like seeing people. That is the time when you should schedule your interviews, reports from subordinates, and open-door period when people can interrupt you. Scheduling this way will avoid feelings of resentment when people interrupt you just as you are getting into an important task.

Perhaps you have a top client or customer who picks up the phone whenever the slightest problem or question comes up. Or it may be that your boss or a subordinate cannot wait to talk with you on matters of slight importance. There are two ways of scheduling these people without offending or alienating them.

First, schedule regular interface—say, once or twice a week. If your contacts know they will see you Wednesday at eleven, they will be more likely to save up their routine questions and needs for the regular time. This meeting can be held by phone if it is more convenient for both parties. Of course, occasional emergencies will crop up between meetings, but the draining away of your time by inconsequential matters should be cut back this way.

Think ahead to others' demands. Get a feel for your client's or boss's needs and be prepared so that a regular need does not become a last-minute demand. If in October your client asks

for some figures for a monthly meeting at his corporate head-
quarters, inquire as to whether such figures will be needed
monthly from now on. If so, schedule them in to your regular
plan; do not wait to be asked in November.

TAKE A DAY OFF

If interruptions are getting you down, take a day off.
Do not stay home, though—go to the conference room at work
or a quiet, private place. Some executives we know rent a
quiet motel room, unplug the television, and put a "Do Not
Disturb" sign on the door. Spend the whole day out of touch
with your usual routines to concentrate on something very big.
You will get a surprising amount accomplished, probably more
than you could ever do in a week of routine coping. And you
will get an instant appraisal of your staff and your office procedures. If you are the indispensable person for everything (in
other words, if the office is in chaos when you return), you are
not set up for maximum effectiveness.

DO NOT BE AFRAID TO PUNT

One pitfall when you get organized and use a To Do
list each day is that you may fear losing flexibility. If you are
interrupted by a chance to have lunch with a prospective client or a crisis on a big project comes up, you may feel that
your day is blown for good.

This does not have to happen if you learn to "punt," or stop
and start over. Stay calm, look at that To Do list, and reorder
those priorities. Then adopt your new, reordered plan immediately so that you will not waste time stewing over the surprise
interruption. You can help yourself prepare for this by num-
bering your projects in order of importance or labeling them
A, B, and C priority right on the To Do list.

HOW TO DISCOURAGE OFFICE VISITORS

Never volunteer to hold a meeting in your office. Try to have it in someone else's office so that you can leave if you have to or want to. Do not get stuck as the host of a meeting. One way to avoid playing host is to rid your office of extra chairs—just keep your own. This discourages drop-in visitors, too.

When someone drops in, keep a phone, pencil, or paper in hand as a sign that you expect to get back to work soon. Ask, "How much of my time do you need?" Look at your clock or, if the interrupter is a frequent time-waster, set an alarm to confirm such a limit.

REROUTE NEEDLESS INTERRUPTIONS

The customer service manager of a large manufacturer gave *Execu-Time* this idea for rerouting misdirected inquiries:

> I used to be swamped with phone calls, letters, and even drop-in visitors seeking information and answers right now. There was not enough time in the day to handle them all, and half of them did not need or want me, anyway. After I realized I could never keep up, I developed a system for rerouting a lot of these inquiries without my even handling them. I compiled a "guidebook" to the company for my secretary. It lists just about every sort of inquiry, and gives the person I think can best handle it. Now my secretary reroutes nearly all these misdirected inquiries, and I have the time I need to adequately handle the complaints that belong in my department.

WHAT TO DO WHEN
A VISITOR WON'T LEAVE

Some people ask their secretaries to buzz them when a predetermined amount of time has elapsed, citing a phone call or another appointment coming up, in order to make a visitor leave. If you do not feel comfortable with this charade, here is an idea from a marketer at a major chemical firm on how to get rid of long-winded visitors: "I was never comfortable having my secretary buzz me to interrupt unwanted drop-ins. But often there's no other way to get free. So now I do it myself. In the middle of the unwanted conversation, I simply pick up the phone and tell my secretary, 'I'll be through here in a minute.' That gets my visitors out of my office, usually for a couple of weeks."

HANDLING DROP-INS

If your business is purchasing, perhaps you schedule a time for "open calling" by salespeople. But if you, like a number of managers, must juggle your purchasing responsibilities with many other jobs, you are being unfair to yourself if you allow salespeople to call on you when it happens to suit them. They will tell you that they were "in the neighborhood and thought they would drop in." You do not have to see them unless you have the time in your schedule or unless you feel they may have an answer you have been searching for.

Make a rule for yourself and stick to it so that those who shield you are not in doubt. Perhaps you will want to be informed when one of your regular suppliers stops in and to make the decision whether to see him, depending upon the work at hand. To be fair to your regular salespeople, explain that you prefer not to be "dropped-in on"; some clients actually like it, and your salesperson may assume you are one of them.

It may well be part of your rule that no salesperson gets a minute of your time unless specifically scheduled in advance. And if salespeople call and say they will be in "sometime today," either get them to make a specific time or instruct your assistant to see them when they show up. Your suppliers must learn that your time is scheduled to your convenience, not theirs.

CUTTING DOWN ON OFFICE NOISE

If you are trying to increase your concentration level and attention span, the noise level in your office may be interrupting you without your even knowing it. If your office is too close to the action outside, you may be bothered by conversations, phones ringing, and even drop-in visitors who get all the way to your door without being intercepted.

If you cannot soundproof your office area, you can at least insist on a closed-door policy for part of the day. And if that does not work, find yourself a hideaway in a spare office or at home where you can concentrate in quiet when the job demands.

THE QUIET HOUR

If you do not schedule yourself at least one quiet hour each day, you are overlooking one of your best opportunities to get your work under control. The basic rules of a quiet hour are these: (1) no phone calls taken or made, (2) no visitors and no leaving your office to see anyone, (3) no unnecessary talking or moving around. These are simple ideas, but a great percentage of managers seldom apply them.

You need a quiet hour to allow for concentrated work without interruptions. Your firm could use a quiet-hour policy, too. The companies that have tried it report great enthusiasm and a measurable jump in management output.

The theory behind the quiet hour is that when you allow yourself to be interrupted (at an average of once every eight minutes unless you do something about it) your work is constantly subject to "gear-up" and "cool-down" times. But when you carve out a quiet hour, you can get started and keep working without all those starts and stops.

A great number of managers choose to have the quiet hour first thing in the morning, because it gets the day off to a productive start. You start the day with a positive attitude, checking off a big "think project" on your To Do list or a whole group of smaller jobs.

The quiet-hour practice helps you get started with other time-management techniques, too. For example, the calls held during your quiet hour can be returned all at once, as suggested in Chapter 4. You can delegate and answer peoples' questions all at one time instead of seeing the same people three or four times in the first hour or so of the day. Furthermore, you will have an added incentive to practice concentration techniques because you will want to get as much as you can out of your hard-won hour of silence.

Most important to implementing a quiet hour is the awareness of your subordinates, fellow workers, and outside contacts of what a quiet hour is, what you do with it, and why you feel it is necessary. Do not let them assume that it is your nap time or some other frivolous use of time.

To get full value from the quiet hour, try to sell the idea to your entire company or department. Explain the rules: no calls, visitors, or unnecessary communication. Ideally, everyone in the office would have a quiet hour at once, with just one receptionist fielding calls and inquiries.

Do not just tell your subordinates, "Now you have a quiet hour." You need to explain what you expect them to do with it. Help them set objectives for organization, planning, and developing new ideas or solutions to problems. Or help them learn to isolate that top-priority project for the day and do it during the quiet hour.

Clerical workers—when they are not taking their turns as receptionist during the quiet hour—can utilize the time to file, catch up on paperwork, and develop better organization systems.

Note the quiet-hour sign on the next page. It makes an ex-

Please come back at

Copyright © 1981 Januz Marketing Communications, Inc.

cellent reminder—especially if you are taking a quiet hour and those around you are not. (Write *Execu-Time*, at the address on page 60, to inquire about copies of the stop sign for your office.)

You can post the sign on your door, the front of your desk, or other prominent place so that those who enter know the quiet hour is on. Make it a point to take down your quiet-hour sign as soon as the time has elapsed, or else the impact and meaning will be lost. You can make your sign reusable by writing the "Please come back at" time in grease pencil or taping the time on.

Like any other office procedure, the quiet hour has to be enforced. Otherwise, enthusiasm and adherence will break down to the point where people will feel it is just a token policy. You also have to be strong enough to make no exceptions. Say an important call comes through and you decide to take it. Next week, the same person may call again during your quiet hour.

Your fellow office workers can slowly slide the quiet hour out of effectiveness, too: whispers become quiet conversations and then full-fledged talkathons, and walks to the water cooler become trips to the cafeteria and then coffee breaks during quiet hour—the list of possible infractions is endless. So renew and rededicate the quiet hour at the first sign of weakness.

Talk with your peers and try to win their support for your quiet-hour concept. If they do not want to try it in their departments, at least try to get them to encourage their people to help you out by avoiding unnecessary infringements on your quiet hour.

Have your own quiet hour even if no one else in the firm will cooperate, by coming in an hour earlier than everyone else, working at lunch time and having lunch at another time, or hiding in the empty conference room, library, or a vacant office for an hour.

Keep demonstrating and recording what the quiet hour is

doing for you. That way, over a period of time, you may be able to win over skeptics who will not listen to your talk about quiet hours but who may be persuaded by facts and figures.

In addition to communicating the facts about your quiet hour within your firm, it helps if you can distribute the information to your suppliers, customers, clients, and so on. Here is a memo that one firm sends out to external contacts:

> This is a reminder that our firm allows staff an uninterrupted morning work period from 8:30 to 10:00. If you try to reach us during those hours, your call will be taken by a telephone answering system. *Please* leave your name and number if you'd like a call back. You can, of course, reach us directly at any time after 10:00 A.M. Thank you.

If you feel as if you really need a full day to catch up on details, why not tell your secretary that you are out of town and either work at home or close the office door and permit absolutely *no interruptions* for the entire day. You will be surprised at how much work you will catch up on.

Quiet-Hour Code Words

Once in a while there will be an emergency that cannot wait until the quiet hour is over. And you would hate to think your top client or the big boss was not able to get through to you when this type of thing came up. You can avoid such a problem by having a secret code word.

One code word could be your full legal name. Or you could pick an official-sounding one such as "Emergency Red." Whatever the term, make sure your secretary or whoever answers the phone during the quiet hour knows what the code word is and that code-worded calls are the only ones that should go through. Be careful: only a few people should have the code word, and they should respect you enough to use it sparingly. Otherwise, you will eliminate your own quiet hour.

Quiet hours for salespeople and other service-oriented people can be accomplished—you just have to work at it a little harder. If you must take customer calls whenever they come in and serve important clients on a moment's notice, try scheduling your quiet hour for the time before the switchboard opens or the hour after it closes at night. Or be "out to lunch" for an hour of quiet.

Early to Rise

A recent study of *Fortune* 500 company chairmen shows that they tend to rise at 6:00 A.M. or earlier. Shouldn't you adopt this habit if you have not already? You can have a home quiet hour and office quiet hour without disturbance. Remember to eat breakfast, though—it is a long time to lunch if you get up at 5:00 A.M. or so.

Cleaning Up

Ever come back to your desk from a meeting or trip and find piles and piles of paper spread around your desk from well-meaning associates who want your attention? And mail, memos, and notes have seemingly sprung from nowhere during your absence.

Here is one way to get the mess cleaned up before you start your quiet hour. Simply take everything and put it in one pile—regardless of the priority of the items. Meanwhile, have your secretary tell associates that you need until a specific time to get organized without interruption. Tack your quiet hour onto this time target when you spread this word; you are sure to need one once the organization process is finished.

Then, take each item in the pile, and decide what to do with it quickly. If the item can be dealt with immediately, put it in the dictation folder or into your own basket for filing. If it requires further attention, it goes into a file folder clearly marked and then into the pending file with a note on your To Do pad.

Then organize your To Do pad. At this point, select the priority item or items for your quiet hour. When you are ready to start the true quiet hour, you can do so in a calm manner because the messiness will be gone. Everything is not yet done, of course, but you will have things under control, and you will be ready to deal with them one by one.

Evaluate Your Quiet Hour

About three months after you initiate the quiet hour, try evaluating it. You can use the results to show skeptics how much quiet hours can do to hype productivity. Use this evaluation system:

Measure output. Ask each participant, on a scale of 0 to 10, how much output has increased over the term of the quiet-hour use.

Measure "roll-over effect." On the same scale, ask each participant to say how well the quiet hour concept extends into other work and time-management aspects—To Do sheets, telephoning, and so on.

Measure enthusiasm. Ask your people to rate their excitement about the quiet-hour concept on a scale of 0 to 10.

If your program scored a totaled average of 0–5 points per person, something is wrong. Are you sure you have followed the quiet-hour guidelines to the letter? If the score averages 6–10 points, keep trying—something positive is happening. If you score 11–20, you are obviously happy with the results. If the score is 21 or above, congratulations—your results are measurable and impressive. Keep up the quiet-hour work and tell your friends.

15.

DEALING WITH STRESS AND CRISIS

Stress is the most widespread executive disease, and one of the most prevalent symptoms of stress is that the victim's time is out of control. Perhaps you have experienced this yourself: You are returning from a meeting or business trip where you were given a number of assignments. Some questions were asked and the answers were not available to you at the time, so you have to look up the answers. You have to set up follow-up meetings with some of the people you saw at this conference. And to top it all off, you know you will be greeted by a stack of phone messages, a desk piled with reports and letters, and a secretary or assistant with lots of projects to talk over with you.

The weight of all these concerns and tasks is great; it may

threaten to overwhelm you. You may have a sinking feeling and be unable to decide what to do first. This is because, at least for the moment, your time is out of control.

Most antistress workshops concentrate on making you relax. But this is only a treatment of the symptom, not a cure. To be cured, you will need to get those tasks and concerns under control—to chart them out, allocate time to each, and perhaps delegate some and eliminate others. This chapter will give you techniques to control emergency situations and overwhelming periods when you cannot seem to get going on a positive course of action.

LIMIT YOUR WORKWEEK

The national average workweek for executives is about fifty-four hours. Some companies seem to have an unofficial contest to see who can come in earliest, leave latest, and take home the fullest briefcase. Other company officers will tell you that the mark of a good manager is to fit everything in between nine and five. A moderate route between the two is most beneficial, we believe. This allows you the extra time to plan and do high-priority think work and still have time for family life, leisure, and relaxation outside your work world. If you cannot see how to cut your workweek below sixty or seventy hours, take a careful look at the techniques in this book—especially the one where you admit to your boss (or to yourself) that you are a human being with limitations.

A CALM RESPONSE TO EMERGENCIES

The best way to avoid emergencies is to plan ahead so that you can anticipate problems and solve them in advance. But when that inevitable emergency or avalanche of work appears, think of yourself as someone working on an emergency ward or in a fire department. Calm, organized, with all necessary tools at hand, such people proceed in an unemotional, rational way to cure the patient or put out the fire. You can plan for this by anticipating types of problems and what your response would be. And keep your tools at hand—phone numbers, addresses, lists of alternative suppliers, and the like so that when an emergency arises you will be prepared.

TAKE FIVE

Another way to control your emotions when a stressful situation occurs is to stop long enough to gain perspective on what is happening. If you think you are entering a crisis, shut the door for five minutes and relax. Let your body go limp and do not think—just let your mind wander for a few minutes.

When you reopen your door, you will have a more rational approach to the crisis at hand; you will be ready to act positively rather than to react emotionally. That way, the crisis can be handled quickly and you can get back to your regular program.

APPROPRIATE CRISIS RESPONSE

Make sure you do not underreact or overreact to a pressurized situation. Try these five steps to determine the correct response and the best action:

Think for five minutes. Do not jump right in doing things willy-nilly. Sit down and evaluate the situation. Is this really a crisis? Is there anything you can do at this point? If not, why stop doing your other work? You cannot afford the luxury of worry over something that cannot be helped. If there is some type of action you can take, stop and look at your To Do Today list. Is this enough of a crisis to bump something off the list of priorities? Even if it is, it may not become your most important job. Make sure you are not guilty of reacting to the pressure of the situation rather than to the importance of the question.

Do not lay blame. If this is a crisis, what good will it do you or anyone else on your team to try to place blame for the situation? Any such evaluation should be done rationally and quietly, and certainly it should be delayed until the crisis has passed. Alienating your fellow workers through name-calling is a time-waster that you may greatly regret.

Think back. Have you had to face a similar situation in the past? What worked then? What did not work? Use your firm's history and your own experience to shed light on the current problem.

Plan a step-by-step program. Allocate your resources carefully, and give each staff member a plan of action. Do not get caught up in details yourself; it is your job to stay in touch with the big picture of the problem.

To combat the crisis effectively, do as little as possible. Big changes and unilateral actions that will be hard to undo are not appropriate at times of stress.

WHAT CAUSES YOUR CRISES?

Even the best organized, most effective time manager can be caught in a crisis from time to time. A trusted supplier may be late all of a sudden, or an error may be overlooked by a usually reliable clerk. These are legitimate emergencies that we all have to face once in a while.

But probably most of the crises we are faced with could be avoided if we could catch them in the "simmering" stage. The way to do this is to learn to recognize the symptoms that precede full-blown crises in your situation. There may be one or more procedures or systems in your organization that are too "loose" for comfort—places where there should be more checks and balances to guard against problems occurring. See if you recognize anything that should be changed in your organization in this list of reasons why crises develop:

Inadequate planning. If you ignore factors that fairly set off alarm bells, if you overplan your days so that you allow no time for reflection and thinking, or if you neglect to look further than a few weeks ahead, inadequate planning could be your problem. Try to catch crises while they are in their early, controllable stages. Plan checks and balances and other control factors to make sure things are being handled properly and that nothing is falling through the cracks.

Estimating time improperly. Maybe you start projects too close to the deadline when you should allow more time for planning and study stages. Or perhaps you just miss the deadlines by a day or two, and should learn to allow a bit more time when you plan things. It could be that you react to each impending deadline as a crisis situation, in which case you should analyze your discomfort with deadlines. Is it that you hate to see a project end? Are you overscheduled, so that you fear deadlines? Learn to estimate deadlines accurately so that you can meet them calmly and with confidence.

Almost enjoying crises. Some people proudly call themselves "firemen"; they relish the challenge of a crisis situation. These types may allow crises to develop when it is not necessary to let the situation go that long. Such acceptance of crisis is a time-waster, because dealing with a problem in the early stages always takes less time than dealing with it in the full-blown crisis stage.

Sweeping things under the rug. If you hold back the facts when a crisis is approaching or try to deny it once it rears its head, face the truth: the problem is not going to go away; in fact, it will probably get worse. Do not be afraid to let your supervisor know when a crisis occurs; it is better to take your medicine at that time rather than take a double dose later for covering the problem up as well.

PREVENTING CRISES

You can begin doing some routine things to help stop crises from occurring. Try these logical steps:

Catalog a set of routine remedies for recurring crises. Once you start this, you will be surprised to find that there is such a thing as a "routine emergency" just as a hospital emergency room treats a number of broken arms and legs. Handle these routine hot spots with a step-by-step procedure prepared in advance.

Delegate responsibility for various types of crises. Evaluate the strengths and weaknesses of your subordinates; some may be the "fireman" type and others may be more methodical. Assign the firemen to the more volatile problems, and ask the methodical types to prevent problems before they start.

Plan alternatives. Make it a practice to anticipate things that could be stumbling blocks to you on each project you undertake. Think about what you would do if anything did go wrong. That way, problems will be just that—problems that can be dealt with by a reasonable plan and not crises that you have to start from scratch to solve.

Worry may well be the worst time thief there is. If you can do something about a problem, figure out the best course of action and get busy. If there is nothing you can do, strive for serenity. Remember that if you could do something directly about the problem, you would. It is all right to be concerned, but it is counterproductive to let worry hinder your ability to work on items that deserve your concentration.

16.

MANAGING HOME
AND FAMILY

D_o not leave your time-management principles at
the office; intelligent use of time is important in your personal
life, too. Some of us have as much stress and crisis management
to deal with at home as we do at the office—especially when
there are teen-agers in the family, little children with constant demands and messes, a troubled marriage, health problems, financial woes, or any number of personal problems to
deal with.

It is not a good idea to let yourself become bogged down by
personal problems and responsibilities any more than you
would allow work problems to control your time. One solution is to take a quiet hour at home, just as you do at the
office.

Everyone needs some time to himself, but busy managers —and especially those in two-career families—must do some real planning to carve out that special time. Perhaps you can plan to get up an hour before anyone else in the family and take that quiet hour to sort out your feelings, plan your day, read for pleasure, or take a restful walk or a brisk jog. These quiet moments will help relieve your tension; constant tension is just as harmful at home as it is in your business life.

Perhaps your home life is fairly harmonious, but your problem is that you feel guilty having fun with the house in disrepair, laundry unwashed, clothes unmended, errands undone, and so on. One solution is to let others do the tedious work.

The others could be your children—if they are old enough to take on more family responsibility—or hired help. Many people tend to write off household help as too expensive and are surprised to find out how little some types of help cost. Why spend an entire weekend washing windows spring and fall when a window-washing service will do it for you for fifty dollars (a recent Chicago price for a four-bedroom house, windows and storms washed inside and out). Unless you enjoy doing your own painting or wallpapering, why do it yourself when wallpapering could be done by outside sources at eight to fourteen dollars a roll for installation, the Midwest range of prices in 1980. The examples abound; the general point is to find out what it would cost to hire someone before you spend your precious free time at tedious chores. You should channel your energies into your work instead and do your best to earn a better living so that you can afford to have others do the jobs you do not enjoy.

For those tasks that you just have to do, try a To Do list for the weekend just as you do for each workday. It does not have to be all work and no play; we suggest that you schedule plenty of time for rest and relaxation. Make an appointment for dinner with your spouse Saturday night, and keep it as scrupulously as you would a business date.

Schedule time for a ball game to balance those two hours spent working on your taxes. Write down a reminder to call your relatives or friends out of town. If you do a bit of advance planning, you will find you can make your weekends full and colorful, refreshing and guilt-free because you will be able to schedule time for work and play and delete the time spent without enjoyment or accomplishment.

CARD-FILE CONTROL

Sisters and disorganized homemakers Pam Brace and Peggy Jones used a system borrowed from Jones's premarriage selling job to get their homes under control. This suggestion may very well work for you and your spouse. Jones had a rotating file of customers and calls to make on a weekly or monthly basis. The same file system works at home for weekly chores such as floor washing, monthly tasks such as bill paying, and such yearly jobs as washing storm windows. You could include break-downs telling which family member is in charge of what; a card file of good service organizations to do cleaning work, repairs, and tune-ups; and a record of how much you have paid for each service or tools to do it yourself.

Sociologist Catherine White Berheide isolated eighty different household tasks as a result of surveys of homemakers in urban areas in various parts of the country. Your list of chores might not run so long when you consider the ages of children, things that do not apply to your family (such as pet care), or items that you have decided are not worth worrying about (careful menu planning, perhaps). Of course, you also may add some chores that others do not have, such as car care and gardening.

Divide the items on your final list into daily, weekly, monthly, and other categories to fit your needs. Set up the file with specific dates for all jobs, and assign jobs to individuals on a regular or rotating basis. Then each day or so you can check the file, do your chores, and then relax, knowing that everything will be covered in due time.

If the number of chores seems a bit overwhelming, consider that most of the cleaning chores could be handled by a one-day-a-week cleaning person who should be available for the minimum wage or a bit more. If you are worried about letting a stranger into your home, especially if you will not be around, consider using a cleaning service; such services are a bit more expensive, but they should be bonded, and they have a lot to lose if there is an incident in your home.

Think once again about which chores you can do yourself and which you really should pay others to do. As one reader of *Execu-Time* put it, "I used to think I was better off to try to do all the home and car repairs myself. I would rationalize buying the tools and materials to help me save time. But I never considered the time it takes to plan the job, get the tools and materials together, do the work, and clean up. Now I have made a list of things I will no longer do but will pay other people to do."

Another pointer for the use of the card-file system is to set it up and play it by ear. If the system is not working, feel free to change it. Perhaps you are bunching all the monthly jobs at the beginning of the month or putting them too close to your most hectic social time of the month. Or maybe you are expecting too much of yourself: is it really necessary to pay bills more than once a month, for instance, or to have all those house plants that need care every week or even more often than that? Try the card file the way you have set it up, but then evaluate and modify it until you achieve a system that works for you and your family.

QUICK TIPS

There are any number of good ideas for organizing your family and home life—not with military precision as the goal but simply for the comfort of knowing that things are taken care of so that everyone can relax. Here are some suggestions you may be able to take advantage of to make your home, family, and personal life more serene:

Use the mails. Why bank or pay bills in person? You can shop by mail or phone, too. If you must go to the store in person, at least call ahead to find out if the store has what you are looking for.

Avoid peak hours. Do your food shopping early in the week instead of over the weekend. Stay home during holiday weekends and do the same on Saturday night; your favorite resort or restaurant will be less crowded and more enjoyable at off-peak times.

Use room service when traveling. In an effort to be thrifty, many people avoid room service, but the extra service charge is well worth the money if you have to be somewhere at an early hour. You can avoid the coffee-shop delays and lines and integrate your breakfast into your dressing and packing time.

Organize your finances. Have a financial corner in your home, and keep all your money-related items there. Stack bills in a "due" folder or file, and set definite times to pay them in a batch—once a month or twice at the most, but no more.

Get children off to a good start. Organization expert and author Stephanie Winston, who wrote *Getting Organized*, advises that you start when your children are very young to teach them the time-saving benefits of organization. For instance, you can attach a picture of socks to your toddler's socks drawer or paint one on it if you like a custom designer touch. Even a three-year-old can use this cue to put laundry away in the proper place. Do not expect complete neatness and order; it is a waste of time to have socks lined up like soldiers anyway.

For older children, a simple To Do list is appropriate for chores, homework, lessons, and scheduled play. If you decide to use the card-file system, you might have each person's name on a different-colored divider within the card file or keep a separate box of cards for each participant.

Choose your service people well. Make sure they are truly time-saving and do not just do what seems expedient. For instance, should your dry cleaner, auto repair shop, and shoe repairman really be in your home neighborhood, or would you be better off dealing with someone near work? Try to find services on your commuting route to save time. Use the same services repeatedly to become a known and valued customer, and you may then be able to get special fast service when you need it.

Do not be glued to the tube. Schedule your television viewing. Limit yourself to a few shows of special merit each week. Do not flop down and watch whatever comes on. You should read something, exercise, or catch up on rest instead.

Keep sets of spare keys. Duplicate keys for your home, car, and office should be kept in a safe, handy place—your briefcase, wallet, or purse. If you misplace your main keys, you will be covered. This is a real time-saver for the absentminded.

Get the family together in the morning. With parents at work and children at school all day and with activities and relaxation scheduled for the evening, it may be difficult for the family to get together and just talk or share things. Try doing this at breakfast. Get up a bit earlier and assign each person a job: the little ones can set the table, older children help cook, and everyone help clean up. Newspapers, television, and radio should be left firmly in the "off" position to encourage conversation. Make sure you start early enough so that everyone can linger a bit, enjoying an oasis of leisure before the hectic day begins.

Forget perfection. Especially where two-career families are concerned, perfection in household management is an outmoded goal. Strive simply to make everything adequately clean, comfortable, and complete.

Keep in touch with the family. Make sure you have a "communications center" in your home so that people going in and out know where to look for the latest family bulletins. The kitchen is the best place or right by the door where everyone comes in. This is where children can leave notes stating their whereabouts and where the day's chores or appointments can be posted.

Bunch your appointments. If you have to sit in the doctor's or dentist's office and wait, make sure you do it only once. Get checkup appointments for yourself and all the children at the same time and do the same for other types of appointments whenever possible.

Anticipate child-care crises. If you have been lucky enough to set up a good child-care arrangement, that is great unless the person gets sick or the weather closes the day-care center for the day. Make sure you have a back-up handy—a stay-at-home parent in your neighborhood who is willing to babysit when you are desperate or a cooperative arrangement of some kind. It saves time and nerves when your best-laid plans go awry at 7:00 A.M.

Teach your family systems and make them practice them. Strange as it may seem to you after years of doing laundry and cooking, everyone has to learn how to do these things properly: you did, from your mother or father or other adult—or by trial and error. So make sure you do not just tell your child to "do a load of laundry" or "clean the bathroom." Take the time to show him or her how it is done, allowing plenty of time for questions. The how-to session will pay off in better results each time your child does the job.

In addition to the system for doing the job, make sure the children understand your time schedule. Teach your children to maintain their rooms, make beds, dust, and vacuum, and come to an understanding with them about how often these things should be done. Do not be too upset if your son feels he should vacuum his room only every two weeks instead of weekly; a fortnightly vacuuming by him is better than a weekly one by you.

Everyone cleans up after snacks. Do not fall into the trap of cleaning up crumbs and wrappers a dozen times a day. If your children and spouse can get their own snacks, they can clean up after themselves.

A system for laundry. Get a laundry cart with three compartments—one each for whites, colors, and delicate items. Train your family to put their clothes in the proper areas, to cut down on sorting.

Shop once a week or less. Some organized people are able to do grocery shopping only every two weeks or so, but if you like fresh produce, plan for a weekly trip. Look for a time that is not crowded—perhaps early in the week and early in the evening, after six and before the after-dinner shoppers arrive. Keep a list in the kitchen of things you need, and invite the family to write down items as they run low.

Have a master list. Make up a list of everything you ever buy in the grocery store, preferably conforming to the layout of the store you shop in. That way, instead of writing out a list each week, you can simply check off the items you need.

Keep paperwork under control. At the very least, sort through your mail and other papers once a week before you create a monster. Make sure bills are put in the "To Be Paid" file. Read school reports, sign, and return. Mark invitation days and times on your calendar. File useless items in the circular file to avoid shuffling them again and again.

Shop only twice a year for clothes. With planning, you can do your major shopping in spring and fall trips to your favorite stores, all at once. Do the same for your children. And use the phone to order standard items you know and like— socks, underwear, pajamas, nylons—for all family members.

Keep repairs under control. When you remove a garment, check it for needed cleaning and repairs and set it aside if such help is needed. Get the item to the cleaner or seamstress; do not hang it up and put off repairs or an important part of your wardrobe will be inoperative.

Do your social calendar every month. Have a social calendar on which you list parties, birthdays, weddings, and activities. At the beginning of the month, list all the presents you will need and buy them, along with wrapping paper and cards, all at once. Or sign up with a gift-buying service at your favorite store and have them take care of such matters for you.

Entertain simply and stay calm. Guests enjoy a relaxed barbecue or buffet much more than a tense seven-course dinner. If you scale down the formality of your entertaining, your guests will probably be relieved and do the same when they return the favor.

Accept invitations selectively. Learn to say no to social engagements that do not interest you. You do not owe it to anyone to spend an evening just being social if you do not find it pleasant. Refuse politely and with thanks; this is much more sincere than a reluctant acceptance.

Schedule idleness on your vacations. Busy executives cannot hope to take whirlwind vacations and return refreshed. The purpose of an executive's vacation is to wind down and get a new perspective on things, so opt for the Caribbean beach vacation rather than the ten-day, eight-country European fling.

Keep your eyes open for household time-management tips. Service magazines and other publications have finally caught on to the fact that a great number of their readers lead superbusy, active business lives. They include more and more articles about time management and shortcuts, so read and use them wisely for a richer, more rewarding home and family life.

17

HEALTH TIPS

The greater part of this book discusses mental processes—how you can get your mind in gear for better time-management practices. But physical fitness, comfort, activity level, and other factors play an important part in good time management, too.

PHYSICAL ACTIVITY
CUTS EMOTIONAL REACTIONS

Deadlines, crisis situations, conflicts with other employees, customers, and salespeople can add up to a stressful day. You need to minimize your mental and emotional reactions to stress by "letting go" with some physical activity each day.

One solution is to spend lunch hours playing racquetball, swimming, jogging, or just taking a brisk walk. If you cannot manage the time for specific physical activity like this, try the tips from stress-management counselors at the Management Institute at the University of Wisconsin:

Squeeze the phone as hard as you can before you hang up after each call. You will rid yourself of harmful muscle tension.

Clasp your hands in front of your chest with arms parallel to the floor. Push as hard as possible. This is another fine tension reliever.

Rest your hands on your desk with your feet about three to four feet away from the desk. With back and arms straight, do a slow push-up. You will feel muscle relief in your back, chest, and shoulders.

Grasp the bottom of your chair as you sit. Use both hands, keeping your feet on the floor and your arms and back straight. Lift up; you will stay seated, but the tension will leave your back and arms.

Take a walk to the washroom, for coffee, or around the block. An hour at your desk without a break is the maximum you should expect from yourself except in special, heavy-concentration situations.

If you allow yourself daily physical outlets like these, you will find that your tension and stress quotients will lower significantly. This means you will be able to deal more rationally with demands on your time, stick to your schedule, and deal with problems and crisis situations without blowing the day because of emotional exhaustion.

ACTION BREAKS

There are some active things you can do as a short release from the day's tension. Each of these breaks is just a three- to five-minute change in routine that will refresh you by activating your body and allowing you to use the muscles that are idle as you sit at your desk.

If you allow oxygen to stimulate your muscles by exercising them, you will be surprised at how you can combat fatigue. You will also find that your mental clarity will stay at a higher level throughout the day if you are active a few times during the day's routine. Try these ideas:

Instead of phoning, walk down the hall with a message once in a while. Granted, the phone call would save more time, but you may need the walk to give you a physical lift.

Instead of more coffee, which may heighten nervousness and even make you too hungry, take a break and walk briskly all around the office. You will go back to your desk feeling fresher.

Instead of staring into space or out the window, get up and run in place for a minute. This really gets the oxygen moving and the blood flowing.

Swear off elevators unless you have to get up or down a score of floors. If you have to go just a few floors, walk briskly up and down stairs.

These action breaks should not be done too quickly. Breathe deeply, walk briskly, stretch your shoulders, and look around. You will find that you can get a new perspective on things with just this kind of a short break.

Next time a problem or question comes up that you cannot get a grip on, take a few minutes to review the situation, the facts, the problem as you see it, and the outcome you would like to have occur. (You know you are stuck on the problem when you find yourself staring into space, being easily distracted by other things, or feeling frustrated.) Once you have recognized the problem and reviewed the facts, take one of the action breaks described earlier. When you return to your desk, work on something else. Subconsciously, you will still be working on the knotty problem. And in almost every case, an answer will come to you within forty-eight hours. Try it—it works!

FITNESS AT YOUR DESK

Here are some short exercises you can do right at your desk. They'll help you keep in shape and keep oxygen flowing to your muscles.

1. Place your feet firmly on the floor, then sit at your desk or table and grab it with both hands. Your thumbs should be on top, fingers under the table. Try to lift the desk or table. Hold the tension for three counts, then relax. Do five repetitions to start, more as you become stronger.
2. Try to lift yourself from your chair, using only your arms. Hold for three counts. Relax, then repeat five times to start, with more as you build stamina.
3. Hold the desk for balance. Lift your legs straight out and hold for the count of three. Return your feet to floor, then repeat as described.

Change hand position so that your thumbs are below and your fingers on top of the table or desk. Do these three exercises all over again in this position.

Try doing all these exercises three times weekly, perhaps in place of an action break.

KNOW YOUR PEAK HOURS

Physical and mental concerns work together to influence your peak work hours, but there are some generalities against which you can measure yourself. They have to do with age but may vary with your physical condition and biological clock.

If you are 18 to 30, you probably start off slowly in the morning and reach your peak after lunch. When traditional office hours end around five, you are probably still going strong.

If you are 31 to 40, you may peak early in the morning and have had it by 2:00 P.M.

If you are 41 to 55, you probably build to a peak in the middle of the morning and then find that your energy tapers off for the rest of the day.

To hit the most people in stride, get them together at 10:30 A.M.

Just as your capability varies during the day, so it varies from day to day. Dr. Dorothy Tennov of the University of Bridgeport, Connecticut, says it even varies from minute to minute. This interesting information becomes problem information when you try to do a task that is above your momentary capability.

Ideally, you will sense your basic capability level at any given time, and try to match the task you do with your lowest possible capability level to accomplish it satisfactorily. Knowing that this fluctuation occurs within you, you should be alert to the fact that you may have to revise your To Do list slightly if you hit a low point just when you are supposed to be doing a top-priority job. By the same token, if you are feeling high on the capability scale, and you are slated to clean your files that hour, seize the opportunity to start something new and important that you have been saving for just such a time.

WORKAHOLISM

Workaholism is defined as an addiction to work. This does not necessarily imply success at that work. In fact, the workaholic is likely to be an underachiever because of obsessive tendencies. Even the successful workaholic should recognize this disease and combat it, because there are more effective ways of working and living.

Workaholics are compulsive about work. They have to be the first one in each morning and the last one out at night. Never mind that fatigue and stress overcome them and make them ineffective for the greater part of the day—these people keep on plugging, no matter what.

The workaholic wastes time and energy on insignificant chores. Classic victims of the "only I can do it" syndrome, they shy away from delegation. In the drive for efficiency and getting a lot done, workaholics neglect to ask whether they are being effective or getting the right things done.

Workaholics lack specific goals. They react rather than act. They put off self-improvement because they are too busy for current undirected activity.

Workaholics undervalue their personal lives; they cancel out of social occasions and disappoint children and spouses. They make work a religion and consider it important above all else.

If you recognize yourself in the above description, it is time to take stock. Start thinking "effective," not just "efficient." Remember the importance of family and friends, and above all, sit down in a quiet, nonstressful environment and plan. Make short-term and long-term plans, and learn to use these carefully made plans as your guide to daily activity.

TWO FINAL REMINDERS

Perhaps these warnings are obvious, but it does not hurt to restate them, because they are so true.

First, smoking can make you lazy, in addition to its being a health threat. The carbon monoxide in smoke makes it more difficult for your blood to carry oxygen. So if you cannot seem to cut down or stop smoking for health reasons, do it to help you manage your time better. Think how much time you will save by not lighting up, puffing, searching for ash trays, and so on.

Second, alcohol is a time-waster. Save your drinking—if you do it at all—for after work, when you can afford to slow down. Remember that alcohol is a depressant. You will work more slowly all afternoon after one or two drinks.

Appendix

TIME-SAVING RESOURCES

NEWSLETTERS

One fine way to keep abreast of new research in time-management techniques and to review important basics on a regular basis is to subscribe to a time-management newsletter such as *Execu-Time*. A short sitting (fifteen minutes or so) twice a month is all you need to reemphasize time management in your own mind by reading up on practical hints and the theories behind them.

Execu-Time. Published twice monthly by Januz Marketing Communications, Inc., P. O. Box 631, Lake Forest, Illinois 60045.

Time Talk. Published monthly by Time-Management Center, P. O. Box 5, Grandville, Michigan 49418.

Chronolog. Published by Guidelines, Box 456, Orinda, California 94563.

CASSETTE TAPES

Douglass, Donna N. *Relaxation Made Easy*
Douglass, Merrill E. Creative Use of Time

Eliminating Timewasters
Finding Time to Manage
How to Conquer Procrastination
How to Organize Your Desk and Handle Your
Paperwork

Individual tapes published by Time-Management Center.

Time Management for Today. Six-cassette tape album. General
Cassette Corporation, 1324 North 22nd Avenue, Phoenix, Arizona 85005.

Getting Things Done, by Ed Bliss. Six-cassette tape album. Ed Bliss,
El Rancho Loma Serena, Mountain Ranch, California 95246.

SEMINARS

If you would like an intensive experience in time-management
learning, be on the lookout for a good seminar in your locale. But
before you go, consider these pointers on getting the most out of
your seminar:

Find out exactly what will be covered. Make sure that the angle
is right for you and your business. To do this, do not just glance
over the descriptive materials but actually study them. Make notes
and see how many of the topics that will be covered fit in with the
goals for learning that you have made for yourself. Think a bit
further to see how many specific applications this material will
have for your day-to-day work.

Get to the seminar early. Skim the course materials to get a
grasp of the subject before the course session begins. Talk with
some of the other attendees so that you can share impressions during breaks and after the seminar is over.

Do not try to learn everything that is taught. Listen carefully for
important ideas and techniques that appeal to you and your circumstances.

Ask questions and join small-group seminars. You get more out
of the program as an active participant.

Practice what you learn step-by-step. Do not go back to the office
and try to implement ten new concepts the first week. Schedule
the items for implementation one at a time over a period of weeks,
months, or even years.

*A few weeks after the program, get out your materials and notes
and review them.* Even better, agree with another seminar participant to get together on a regular basis every month or so for a year

to cover the ground again and again until you have reaped every ounce of wisdom you can from the materials presented.

Here are six time-management training organizations with top credentials and proven track records. Contact them at the addresses and phone numbers listed for course outlines and a list of upcoming seminar dates and locations.

Ed Bliss, El Rancho Loma Serena, Mountain Ranch, California 95246, (209) 754–3560

Bliss devotes the first half of his excellent *Getting Things Done* seminar to nuts-and-bolts problems, such as paperwork, interruptions, structuring a day, etc., and the last half to psychological factors, such as enhancing time awareness and dealing with the wheel-spinning syndrome. He does mostly in-house seminars but has several continuing programs with universities and associations.

Merrill Douglass, Time-Management Center, 3733 Omaha, Grandville, Michigan 49418, (616) 531–1870

This creative thinker presents a well-paced program with lots of "hows" and "whys" for time managers. He concentrates on human weaknesses and how to overcome them for better time management, with lots of help to cope with interruptions and time-wasters. In-house programs by arrangement are his specialty, but Douglass offers some public programs sponsored by business schools or management-training associations.

John Lee, Hour Power, Inc., Lake Ellen Executive Center, Box 398, Crawfordville, Florida 32327, (904) 926–7121

Lee is a captivating speaker with a forceful style. He has some impressive hard data to present, along with some how-to techniques for time management. His specialty is the biological factor —that is, using your own natural "body time" to find peak periods and valleys. He runs mostly in-house programs by prior arrangement but has a regular schedule of public seminars, sponsored locally by chambers of commerce.

Alec MacKenzie, Box 130, Greenwich, New York 12834, (518) 692–9626

Known for his scholarly approach, MacKenzie is also dynamic and compelling as a speaker. He stresses participation by seminar attendees and does his best to help each individual relate learning to everyday business and home challenges. In-house programs comprise a good part of MacKenzie's schedule, but he does a number of his own programs nationally and internationally, in addition to some programs sponsored by management-training organizations. If you set up a special program or plan to attend a MacKenzie seminar, confirm that he himself will be the speaker rather than one of his associates.

Fred Pryor, P. O. Box 2951, Mission, Kansas 66202, (913) 384–6400

This smooth, quick-witted speaker is a real entertainer whose time-management seminar is an enjoyable experience. His program is recommended for team attendance, as it raises consciousness levels about problems and opportunities in time management. The Pryor schedule includes a large number of public programs across the country on a regular basis.

Robert D. Rutherford, 1195 Fairfield Drive, Boulder, Colorado 80303, (303) 447–0360

Rutherford's two main themes are "concentration on high-payoff activities" and "wanting time management to work." His presentation has a delayed reaction that allows the fruits of his message to ripen over time. He does some in-house work, but the greater part of his schedule comprises public programs on a national basis and a group of programs run by a California university.

FILMS

To initiate your employees into the concept of time management, you might consider a time-management film. Check with business film sources for a film to fit your audience. Such a film could serve as the stepping off point for a new time-management program in your firm. Here are some suggested films.

A Perfectly Normal Day. Cally Curtis Company, 711 3rd Avenue, New York, NY

A Team of Two. Cally Curtis Company

Managing Time, with Peter Drucker. BNA, 1095 2nd Avenue, New York, NY

The Time of Your Life. Cally Curtis Company

Time and Territory Management. Dartnell Corporation, 4660 N.
   Ravenswood Avenue, Chicago, IL
Time and Territory Management, with Joe Batten. BNA
Time Is Money. Cally Curtis Company
Time to Think. Rank-Roundtable
Time Well Spent. Rank-Roundtable

OTHER RESOURCES

Many other services and types of equipment may come in handy
as time-savers for you if you keep your eyes and ears open for them.
Library research services, heads of special-interest associations,
government agencies, and other sources may be able to save you a
great deal of time and effort in finding information, for instance.
And if you read the *Wall Street Journal, Execu-Time,* and other
business-oriented publications, you will learn about new sources
and types of equipment that save time, directly or indirectly.

The *Management Inventory on Time Management* can help you
and your staffers evaluate present time use and get ideas on how to
improve it. Written by Donald L. Kirkpatrick, professor of management development at the University of Wisconsin, the inventory is
available in the form of a preview copy of the sixty-question test.
Each question relates to a time-management problem and asks you
to "agree" or "disagree." The answer key offers discussion points
that could lead to a lively exchange among your staff members. To
obtain the preview copy of the "inventory," write to Donald Kirkpatrick at University of Wisconsin Extension, 929 N. 6th Street,
Milwaukee, Wisconsin 53202, and mention this book.

Bibliography

BOOKS

Armstrong, Richard. *The Time of Your Life*. New York: Christo-
phers, 1977.

Auger, B. Y. *How to Run Better Business Meetings*. New York:
Amacom, 1972.

Baer, J. L., and H. Fensterheim. *Don't Say Yes When You Want to
Say No*. New York: McKay, 1975.

Becker, Selwyn W. *The Efficient Organization*. New York: Elsevier,
1975.

Benson, Herbert. *The Relaxation Response*. New York: Morrow,
1975.

Bliss, Edwin. *Getting Things Done*. New York: Scribners, 1976.

Bloch, Arthur. *Murphy's Law*. Los Angeles: Price, Stern, Sloan,
1977.

Cooper, Joseph. *How to Get More Done in Less Time*. Rev. ed.
New York: Doubleday, 1971.

Davidson, James. *Effective Time Management.* New York: Human Sciences, 1978.

Dayton, Edward R. *Tools for Time Management.* Grand Rapids, Mich.: Zondervan, 1974.

Dobyns, Richard C., and R. L. Dobyns. *Time: The Irretrievable Asset.* Watsonville, Ca.: Correlan, 1973.

Douglass, Merrill E. *Timely Time Tips.* Grandville, Mich.: Time Management Center, 1975.

———. *How to Control the Time of Your Life.* New York: Norton, 1978.

———, and Donna N. Douglass. *Manage Your Time, Manage Yourself.* New York: AMAcom, div. of Amer. Mgt. Assn.,1980.

Drucker, Peter. *People and Performance.* New York: Harper and Row, 1977.

Dunsing, Richard J. *You and I Have Got to Stop Meeting This Way.* New York: American Management Assn., 1978.

Engstrom, Ted, and R. Alec MacKenzie. *Managing Your Time.* Grand Rapids, Mich.: Zondervan, 1967.

Fanning, Tony, and Robbie Fanning. *Get It All Done and Still Be Human.* Radnor, Pa.: Chilton, 1979.

Feldman, Edwin B. *How to Use Your Time and Get Things Done.* New York: Fell, 1968.

Frailey, Lester E. *Handbook of Business Letters.* West Nyack, New York: Prentice-Hall, Inc., 1965.

Goldfein, Donna. *Everywoman's Guide to Time Management.* Millbrae, Calif.: Les Femmes, 1977.

Grossman, Lee. *Fat Paper.* New York: McGraw-Hill, 1978.

Herzberg, F. *The Managerial Choice.* Homewood, Ill.: Irwin, 1976.

Longeward, Dorothy, and Muriel James. *Born to Win.* New York. NAL, 1978.

Kelly, Al. *What to Do and What Not to Do to Make Life Easier for Yourself at Work.* New York: McGraw-Hill, 1973.

Kiev, Ari. *A Strategy for Daily Living.* New York: Free Press, 1973.

———, Laird, Donald A., and Eleanor C. Laird. *The Techniques of Delegating.* New York: McGraw-Hill, 1957.

Lakein, Alan. *How to Get Control of Your Time and Your Life.* New York: Wyden, 1973.

Lebhar, M. Godfrey. *Use of Time.* New York: Lebhar-Friedman, 1958.

Le Boeuf, Michael. *Working Smart.* New York: McGraw-Hill, 1980.

Lehrer, Robert N. *Work Simplification.* Englewood Cliffs, N.J.: Prentice-Hall, 1972.

Le Tourneau, Richard. *Management Plus.* Grand Rapids, Mich.: Zondervan, 1976.

Lieberman, H., and Erwin Rausch. *Managing and Allocating Time: Industrial.* Cranford, N.J.: Didactic Systems, 1976.

Loen, Raymond. *Manage More by Doing Less.* New York: McGraw-Hill, 1971.

Love, Sydney. *Mastery and Management of Time.* Englewood Cliffs, N.J.: Prentice-Hall, 1978.

McClelland, David. *The Achievement Motive.* New York: Appleton, 1953.

McConkey, Dale. *No-Nonsense Delegation.* New York: American Management Assn., 1974.

McGill, Michael E. *The 40 To 60 Year Old Male.* New York: Simon and Schuster, 1980.

McKay, James T. *The Management of Time.* Englewood Cliffs, N.J.: Prentice-Hall, 1958.

MacKenzie, R. Alec. *New Time-Management Methods for You and Your Staff.* Chicago: Dartnell, 1975.

———. *The Time Trap.* New York: Amacom, 1972.

Maltz, Maxwell. *Psycho-Cybernetics.* Englewood Cliffs, N.J.: Prentice-Hall, 1960.

Marcus, Jay B. *The TM and Business.* New York: McGraw-Hill, 1977.

Mintzberg, Henry. *The Nature of Managerial Work.* New York: Harper and Row, 1973.

Newman, William H. *Administrative Action.* Englewood Cliffs, N.J.: Prentice-Hall, 1963.

Nichols, Ralph, and Leonard Stevens. *Are You Listening?* New York: McGraw-Hill, 1957.

Odiorne, George. *Management and the Activity Trap.* New York: Harper and Row, 1974.

One Hundred Fifty-Five Office Shortcuts and Time Savers for the Secretary. Englewood Cliffs, N.J.: Parker Publishing, 1973.

Parkinson, C. Northcote. *Parkinson's Law.* Boston: Houghton Mifflin, 1957.

Ross, Joel E. *Managing Productivity.* West Nyack, N.Y.: Management Books Institute, 1977.

Rothery, Brian. *How to Organize Your Time and Resources.* New York: Beekman, 1972.

Schaill, William S. *Seven Days to Faster Reading.* Hollywood: Wilshire Book Company, n.d.

Sloma, Richard S. *No-Nonsense Management.* New York: Macmillan, 1977.

Smith, Manuel J. *When I Say No I Feel Guilty.* New York: Dial, 1975.

Stein, Mark L. *The T Factor.* New York: Playboy, 1977.

Tanner, Ogden, *et al. Stress.* Alexandria, Va.: Time-Life, 1976.

The Time Management Workbook. Grandville, Mich.: Time Management Center, 1980.

Uris, Auren. *The Efficient Executive.* New York: McGraw-Hill, 1957.

Van Fleet, James. *Twenty-Two Biggest Mistakes Managers Make and How to Correct Them.* Englewood Cliffs, N.J.: Prentice-Hall, 1973.

Vizza, Robert F. *Time and Territory Management for the Salesman.* New York: Sales Executive Club, 1971.

Webber, A. Ross. *Time and Management.* New York: Van Nostrand Reinhold, 1977.

Wilson, Howard. *Utilizing Time Effectively Through Better Management Processes.* Irvine, Ca.: Administrative Research Associates, Inc., 1973.

ARTICLES

Adcock, Robert L., and John W. Lee. "Time, One More Time." *California Management Review,* Winter 1971.

Arnold, John D. "The Chin-Down Manager." *Fortune,* July 1974.

Barrett, F. D. "Everyman's Guide to Time Management." *Business Quarterly,* Spring 1973.

Burkholder, Robert A. "It's Results That Count." *Journal of Systems Management,* November 1974.

Collicoat, Stephen. "Shorter Hours for Top Executives." *Management Review,* April 1973.

Cook, Melvin. "Measuring Work That's Hard to Measure." *Supervisory Management,* September 1967.

Douglass, Merrill E. "Creative Use of Time." *Personnel Administrator,* October 1975.

———. "Organizing Your Desk and Your Paperwork." *Ibid.,* January 1976.

———. "Test Your Assumptions About Time Management." *Ibid.,* November 1976.

―――. "Stress and Personal Performance." *Ibid.*, August 1977.

―――. "Managing Time Effectively." *Atlanta Economic Review*, May–June 1978.

―――. "How to Conquer Procrastination." *Advanced Management Journal,* Summer 1978.

Drucker, Peter. "How Effective Executives Use Their Time." *Management Review*, October 1967.

Gordon, Mitchell. "How Businessmen Save Time." *Management Review*, November 1966.

Gordon, Paul. "Formula for a 70-Minute Hour." *Business Horizons,* Spring 1961.

Green, Thad. "Time Out for Management." *Manage,* January–February 1976.

Heywood, James D. "Manage Your Time by Managing Your Activities." *Supervisory Management,* May 1974.

Hinrichs, John R. "Where Has All the Time Gone?" *Personnel,* July–August 1976.

Hogue, W. Dickerson. "What Does Priority Mean?" *Business Horizons,* December 1970.

Jackson, John R., and Roger L. Hayen. "Rationing the Scarcest Resource: A Manager's Time." *Personnel Journal,* October 1974.

James, William. "Making Habits Work for You." *Reader's Digest,* August 1967.

Jay, Antony. "How to Run a Meeting." *Harvard Business Review,* March–April 1976.

Jones, Curtis H. "The Money Value of Time." *Harvard Business Review,* July–August 1968.

Kobert, Norman. "How Smart Executives Save Time." *Boardroom Reports,* Sept. 15, 1977.

Lee, John W. "Eleven Ways to Make the Time You Need." *Association Management,* April 1973.

MacKenzie, R. Alec. "Toward a Personalized Time Management Strategy." *Management Review,* February 1974.

―――. "Educational Administrator's Time Management—A Message for All?" *Business Quarterly,* Summer 1976.

Mee, John. "The Zeigarnik Effect (Compulsion to Task Completion)." *Business Horizons,* June 1969.

Mintzberg, Henry. "The Manager's Job: Folklore and Fact." *Harvard Business Review,* July–August 1975.

Morrow, Winston V., Jr. "Can You Be More Efficient?" *Industry Week*, Mar. 12, 1973.

Murrah, Charles R. "How to Get on Top of Your Job." *Nation's Business*, April 1971.

Oncken, William, Jr., and Donald L. Wass. "Management Time: Who's Got the Monkey?" *Harvard Business Review*, November–December 1974.

Rice, Paul L. "Making Minutes Count." *Business Horizons*, December 1973.

Schaffer, Robert H. "Demand Better Results—and Get Them." *Harvard Business Review*, November–December 1974.

Schindall, Henry. "How to Get Rid of a Bulging Briefcase." *Business Management*, January 1964.

Stein, Barry; Allan Cohen; and Herman Gadon. "Flextime: Work When You Want To." *Psychology Today*, June 1976.

Strong, Lydia. "Of Time and Top Management." *Management Review*, June 1956.

Trickett, Joseph A. "A More Effective Use of Time." *California Management Review*, Summer 1962.

"Triumph of Trivia." *Management Review*, October 1968.

Uris, Auren. "Make Your Time More Productive." *Nation's Business*, April 1963.

Webster, Eric. "How to Make the Best Use of Time." *International Management*, September 1971.

"Why Procrastinate?" *Royal Bank of Canada Monthly Letter*, November 1959.

Wilkinson, William R. "Don't Spend Time—Invest It." *Michigan Business Review*, July 1974.

Young, Thomas C. "Managing Time: How to Get the Most Out of Each Working Day." *Association Management*, May 1975.